MULTIPLE PERSPECTIVES IN PERSISTENT BULLYING

Multiple Perspectives in Persistent Bullying: Capturing and listening to young people's voices recognizes that bullying plays a significant role in influencing the social, emotional, physical and cognitive wellbeing of many children and young people. The authors of this insightful text question what reinforces and perpetuates persistent bullying despite intensive interventions and suggest proactive strategies to address this phenomenon. Multiple perspectives on persistent bullying are provided by giving voice to those who bully, are victimized, are both bully and victim and those who desist their bullying behaviour. This book foregrounds these voices to gain new insights into the characteristics of those who persistently bully and the mechanisms that reinforce their behaviour. Examples drawn on include discussions of turning points, teacher expectancy theory and self-verification.

Multiple Perspectives in Persistent Bullying: Capturing and listening to young people's voices includes international research that explores bullying in relation to education, psychology and social media, with implications for policy and practice. It is a crucial and fascinating read for anyone wishing to gain insight into the lives of those who are victimized or bully and find proactive support measures involving all stakeholders. These multiple perspectives will inform future school-based interventions and serve to improve the life trajectories and wellbeing of students, their peers and the school community.

Deborah Green is Lecturer in Humanities and Social Sciences at the Division of Education, Professional Communities Co-ordinator and member of the Centre for Research in Education's Wellbeing Research Group, University of South Australia.

Deborah Price is Program Director, Master of Teaching, Lecturer in Inclusive Education and Wellbeing and Deputy Director of the Centre for Research in Education's Wellbeing Research Group, University of South Australia.

MULTIPLE PERSPECTIVES IN PERSISTENT BULLYING

Capturing and listening to young people's voices

Deborah Green and Deborah Price

Routledge
Taylor & Francis Group

LONDON AND NEW YORK

First published 2017
by Routledge
2 Park Square, Milton Park, Abingdon, Oxon OX14 4RN

and by Routledge
711 Third Avenue, New York, NY 10017

Routledge is an imprint of the Taylor & Francis Group, an informa business

© 2017 D. M. Green and D. A. Price

British Library Cataloguing in Publication Data
A catalogue record for this book is available from the British Library

Library of Congress Cataloguing in Publication Data
A catalog record for this book has been requested

ISBN: 978-1-138-96106-7 (hbk)
ISBN: 978-1-138-96108-1 (pbk)
ISBN: 978-1-315-66001-1 (ebk)

Typeset in Bembo
by Out of House Publishing

Printed and bound by CPI Group (UK) Ltd, Croydon, CR0 4YY

This book is dedicated to our supportive families who have walked every step of the way with us in our quest to reduce bullying globally by gaining a deeper understanding of those who persistently bully.

I wish to thank my wonderful daughter, Nicole, who has supported me with love, encouragement and an endless belief that I can change the lives of those who engage in persistent bullying. Nicole is such a special and inspirational person and unknowingly has provided me with the motivation to persevere so that this book may become a reality. I would also like to thank my own parents, Rosaline and Richard, who provided endless guidance and support throughout my life. I dedicate this book to Nicole, and to the memory of my dear father who I miss more than words can say. Finally, I would also like to thank and acknowledge the contribution, passion, friendship and collegiality of my co-writer and co-researcher Deborah Price – together we have achieved so much. Without you this book would not be possible.

Deborah Green

I dedicate this book to my daughters Alexandra, Isabelle and Bridgette for their unconditional love and support and for continually challenging people to genuinely listen to the multiple perspectives of young people in order to seek a deeper understanding of the complexities in their everyday lives. I would also like to acknowledge the incredible strength of my husband Jamie, who has prioritized the safety, wellbeing and achievement of young people with disabilities and constantly advocates for their voices to be valued. I would also like to thank my parents Marlene, Allen and Barry who have instilled in me a caring nature and passion for the inclusion and wellbeing of others. Finally, I commend my co-author and dear friend Deborah Green, for her resilience, generosity and inspiration in advocating for deeper understanding in relation to persistent bullying.

Deborah Price

We also dedicate this book to the young people, parents, caregivers, educators and members of the broader educational sector who together are working to increase inclusive practices and reduce persistent bullying. In particular, we treasure the voices and lived experiences shared through *Multiple Perspectives in Persistent Bullying: Capturing and listening to young people's voices.*

CONTENTS

FOREWORD

This is an innovative and original book that explores the issue of persistent bullying. This is not an easy task, but Deborah Green and Deborah Price have succeeded by eliciting the perspectives of children and young people who are involved in some way with such bullying – whether as victims, bullies, bystanders or outsiders – through accounts of their lived experiences of this disturbing phenomenon. The authors have succeeded in winning the trust of their participants in such a way as to enable these young people to explain the issue from their own perspectives. This phenomenological study could not have been achieved without the authors' evident love and respect for children, and genuine wish to understand their worlds.

The authors also discuss the recent emergence of a new form of bullying: cyberbullying. They explore its overlap with traditional forms of bullying as well as its unique characteristics. In this book we hear the voices of those young people who are persistently bullied over time and the anguish that they experience. Just as importantly, we hear the voices of those who persistently bully, and we gain significant insights into why they engage in such behaviour. The reader discovers the crucial role to be played by the bystanders, whether they stand by and watch or actively create support mechanisms for the victims and opportunities for the bullies to stop. We also read about turning points in the young people's lives when they were able to break free from the cycle of negative behaviour in which they were trapped. Chapter 1 contains expressive drawings by children of different ages which graphically indicate the power imbalance between bully and victim, the callous disregard for the feelings of a bullied child, and the potential capacity of the group to exclude a fellow student, both physically and psychologically.

The results of the authors' painstaking research are presented systematically and findings discussed in detail, particularly in light of the theoretical models. There are very useful implications for practice that arise from this research and helpful explanations for the apparent 'immunity' or 'resistance' of persistent bullies to the wide range of interventions and sanctions that schools regularly use. I believe that this book heightens awareness of the particular reasons that underlie the bully's thoughts and behaviour. In the process, the authors provide very useful guidelines for schools to modify their practice.

Throughout, the authors show their familiarity with the huge literature on bullying, yet present this knowledge in a readable style that challenges the reader to reflect. We come away from this book with a deeper understanding of the social and psychological processes that underlie bullying. The authors help us to keep a balance between the psychological characteristics of individuals involved in persistent bullying, and the social contexts in which the young people and their peer groups are embedded.

Throughout, the authors advocate the need to work with the *relationship* in order to help those who bully, those who are bullied, and those who are bystanders, to achieve a more creative, person-centred way of being with one another.

Helen Cowie, Emeritus Professor
Faculty of Health and Medical Sciences, University of Surrey

ACKNOWLEDGEMENTS

We wish to acknowledge Anne Morrison for her dedication and commitment to this book. Her collegial approach and editorial expertise have brought this book to fruition. We also acknowledge the research participants who have contributed to the research underpinning each chapter. In particular, the voices of the children and young people who are presented in this book have been pivotal in understanding persistent bullying from multiple perspectives. Without their honesty, time and willingness to share often difficult experiences, this book, and our quest to gain insights into persistent bullying, would not have been a reality. We also acknowledge the expert knowledge and inspiration of Dr Barbara Spears and Emeritus Professor Bruce Johnson as Doctoral supervisors and the contribution of research teams who have a vested interest in improving the wellbeing of students around the world. These researchers include Dr Barbara Spears, Emeritus Professor Bruce Johnson, Dr Margaret Scrimgeour, Alan Barnes and Dr Ruth Geer, who have worked alongside us in a University of South Australia Divisional Research Performance Fund Project titled *Cyber bystanders: The role of the bystander in cyberspace and cyberbullying in an Australian context*.

We also acknowledge the international blind peer reviewers who scrutinized each chapter and provided rigorous feedback and critique. Particularly, we thank Emeritus Professor Helen Cowie for her encouragement, constructive feedback and willingness to write the inspiring Foreword to our book.

PART I
Introduction

1

YOUNG PEOPLE'S PERCEPTIONS OF BULLYING

Some bullies might stop, some bullies may stay the same or others may get worse because they are like 'addicted'.

(Thirteen-year-old girl)

Schools should be safe and fun learning environments where students make friends and interact with peers. Yet often this is not the case due to the impact of bullying. Although the effects of bullying are most detrimental for bullies and victims, other members of the peer group and school community are also negatively affected (Green 2015). Understanding bullying is important because the effects can be significant. For example, students who are persistently victimized may experience internalizing problems such as anxiety, mental health difficulties and, in extreme cases, suicide (Baldry & Winkel 2003). Likewise, those who persistently bully describe elevated risks in the individual, parent, peer and relationship domains, and may experience long-term negative outcomes as a result of their behaviour. While some bullies decrease or desist their actions, *persistent* bullies are immune to interventions and sanctions employed by schools and continue to bully throughout their school life. Of concern, persistent bullies are more likely to have a criminal conviction in adulthood (Olweus 1995; Pepler, Jiang, Craig & Connolly 2008) and, like victims, are at a greater risk of experiencing mental health difficulties and suicidal thoughts (Hinduja & Patchin 2010; Kim & Leventhal 2008; Kumpulainen, Räsänen & Puura 2001; Sampson 2002). Given the widespread impact, it is important to hear the voices of *all* young people involved in the phenomenon of persistent bullying, regardless of the role they may play.

Childhood bullying is considered a socially unacceptable form of aggression often described as:

> [a] physical, verbal or psychological attack or intimidation that is intended to cause fear, distress or harm to the victim; an imbalance of power (psychological or physical) with a more powerful child (or children) oppressing less powerful ones; and repeated incidents between the same children over a prolonged period.
>
> (Farrington & Ttofi 2009, p. 282)

This behaviour is actively discouraged in schools globally, with interventions designed to reduce the prevalence of bullying and to promote young people's safety and wellbeing. Despite these interventions, some individuals persist in bullying, particularly those who increase the behaviour over time or who consistently bully at moderate or high levels (Pepler et al. 2008). These individuals continually challenge interventions while adversely affecting the mental health, wellbeing and schooling experiences of their peers (Bond, Carlin, Thomas, Rubin & Patton 2001; Kaltiala-Heino, Rimpelä, Marttunen, Rimpelä & Rantanen 2000; Olweus 1993).

Multiple Perspectives in Persistent Bullying: Capturing and listening to young people's voices aims to provide insight into why some students persistently bully despite extensive interventions. The intention is to engage international researchers, clinicians and educators (including educational leaders, teachers, school counsellors and higher education providers) in advancing the understanding of individual experiences through critical exploration of the complexities and turning points experienced in addressing persistent bullying. Underpinning this book are the voices and lived experiences of those who persistently bully, are relentlessly targeted, or are seemingly uninvolved. These first-hand accounts share personal and complex insights in relation to persistent bullying.

Part I, Chapter 1: *Young people's perceptions of bullying*, begins by exploring contemporary understandings of bullying before turning specifically to how bullying is perceived by young people. Part II moves to critically explore the lived experiences through *the voices of those who are victimized*. It begins with Chapter 2 and *Leah (victim)*, who expresses her narrative as a young student and her experiences of being bullied by her peers. This is followed in Chapter 3 by a case study of *Brooke* who, as a young adult, reflects on her school life which was fraught with *persistent victimization*. Through Leah and Brooke's lived experiences we identify turning points and chain reactions as a means of further understanding persistent bullying. Part III turns to *the voices of those who bully*, commencing with Chapter 4, in which *Abbie (bully/victim)* shares her lived experiences as a student who was victimized in some circumstances and yet bullied her peers in other situations. Chapter 5 presents the voice of *Rebecca (bully)*. A self-reported bully since commencing school, Rebecca shares with the reader her perspective. This is followed by Chapter 6, in which *John (persistent bully)* provides a retrospective view of a young man who engaged in bullying throughout his school life. John's unique narrative sheds light on the perspective of a persistent bully, which is a relatively unexplored field. While victims and bullies have traditionally been deemed to be the central players in bullying situations, Part IV moves to capture *the voices of those who are uninvolved*. Chapter 7 critically examines the turning points and chain reactions which enabled *Samantha (desister)* to stop bullying, a behaviour that she had engaged in since the commencement of school and yet stopped by Year 4. Of particular interest, Chapter 8 turns to capture the voice of *Bystanders* – the majority of the student population who are present in bullying situations, but stand by as events unfold. Analysing their decisions – whether or not to act – provides a valuable perspective in addressing persistent bullying. Expanding on the bystander insight, Chapter 9 explores the notion of *Cyber and hybrid bystanders* who move between face-to-face and online environments. Having captured the voices of those who are affected by bullying experiences, Part V considers the issues involved in *addressing the problem*. Chapter 10, *Relationships, wellbeing and bullying*, attends to the key role of relationships and the complex interplay between bullying and the wellbeing of victims, bullies, bystanders and the school community. This is followed by Chapter 11, *Turning points and chain reactions*, where we propose a new lens and unique theory which may help to explain persistent bullying. The book concludes with Chapter 12, *Educational implications*, which synthesizes the multiple perspectives on persistent bullying and integrated theories to propose proactive educational measures involving all school community stakeholders. Given that the wellbeing and achievement of every student is the core responsibility of educators globally, gaining insights and understanding through multiple perspectives on persistent bullying is foundational.

Multiple Perspectives in Persistent Bullying: Capturing and listening to young people's voices relies on extensive research in the field of bullying, while drawing on three distinct research projects. The first project involved students across nine South Australian schools and considered their perspectives on bullying and persistent bullying (Green 2015). The second project involved case studies of ten participants recruited from two sites: (1) a Reception–Year 12 school in South Australia; and (2) the University of South Australia's pre-service teacher education programmes (Green 2015). These participants self-identified as bully, victim, bully/victim, desister or bystander and provided insight into their experiences. The third project draws on the voices of 961 students from a South Australian secondary school (Years 8–12, mean age of 15 years). These students were involved in a research study titled *Cyber-bystanders: The role of the bystander in cyberspace and cyberbullying in an Australian context* (Spears, Johnson, Scrimgeour, Barnes, Geer, Price & Green 2009/2010). They provided deep insight into their responses to viewing a digital animation of a typical cyberbullying scenario of a fight that was filmed and uploaded to YouTube. Before turning to the perceptions of those young people who are at the centre of bullying experiences, it is important to outline past and current research understandings of bullying.

Bullying from a researcher perspective

Initially known as '*mobbing*' or '*mobbning*' (the Swedish translation for bullying), research into the area of bullying is extensive and spans decades (Olweus 1978; Smith, Madsen & Moody 1999, p. 8). Prior to this, research focused on aggression: behaviour intended to cause harm to someone who is motivated to avoid it. In the 1960s and early 1970s, it was established that 'mobbing' differed from aggression whereby the latter included a large group or crowd of people who were involved in a common negative activity (Salmivalli 2010). In this early stage, researchers accepted that 'mobbing' was a group phenomenon; a thread remaining in literature over time (e.g. Craig, Pepler & Atlas 2000; Salmivalli, Lagerspetz, Björkqvist, Österman & Kaukiainen 1996; Sentse, Scholte, Salmivalli & Voeten 2007). It became apparent that bullying did not evolve in a vacuum and, as such, Salmivalli and colleagues (1996) identified a number of participant roles: the *bully* who instigates the bullying behaviour; the *follower* who joins in after the bullying has begun; the *reinforcer* who is not actively involved but reinforces by watching, laughing and encouraging the behaviour; the *outsider* who is uninvolved; the *defender* who helps the victim; and the *victim* who is the target of the behaviour.

Over time, Olweus identified the need to clarify the term 'mobbing'. Smith et al. (1999) argued that this term failed to acknowledge individual contributions. Consequently, a more specific term, *bullying*, evolved. Olweus defined this new term as 'systematic one-on-one attacks of a stronger child against a weaker child' (Smith, Cowie, Olafsson & Liefooghe 2002). The focus at this point was primarily on children who engaged in bullying behaviour. Despite no universally agreed definition, most researchers concur that bullying involves repeated acts that are intended to cause harm to the victim who is less powerful. Attributes such as repetition and power have remained constant since Olweus' (1996) earlier definition, and are used by researchers to differentiate bullying from aggression.

In the 1990s, researchers explored various individual characteristics of bullies (e.g. Bernstein & Watson 1997; Hazler, Carney, Green, Powell & Jolly 1997; Olweus 1991, 1994) and victims (Boulton & Smith 1994; Olweus 1978, 1993; Schwartz, Dodge & Coie 1993). During this time, little attention was paid to the interplay between individuals and their environments, yet in 2006 Pepler suggested that more focus needed to be placed on relationships, proposing that bullying is a relationship problem requiring relationship solutions. This focus changed the way researchers and schools looked at bullying. Until this point, a deficit approach focused on what was wrong with the individual, their families and schools, and punitive measures were adopted for bullies. In contrast, the new positive approach focused on identifying and improving relationship difficulties and providing individuals with lifelong skills which involved scaffolding students and changing the social dynamic in which bullying occurs. To fully achieve and sustain such measures, this book prioritizes the critical role of the student voice in order to understand their lived experiences.

How do children understand bullying?

To develop our understanding of bullying, we give voice to young people who are at the forefront of this social phenomenon, either as active participants or as witnesses. As part of a larger study (Green 2015), 113 Reception–Year 9 students across nine South Australian school sites were asked to draw a picture to illustrate their understanding of bullying. This approach offered all students a voice regardless of age or literacy levels and provided insight into the three constructs of bullying: intent, power and repetition. The following drawings indicate young people's awareness and understandings of these constructs.

Intent

The intentional nature of bullying was illustrated by the use of speech bubbles in young people's drawings. For example, in Figure 1.1, a fifteen-year-old boy used the words '*ha ha I got him*'. The smile on the face of the bully as the victim expresses physical pain, exclaiming '*owwch*', infers the bully's intention to hurt.

In Figure 1.2, a nine-year-old girl also used the words '*ha ha you fell over ha ha*', which may imply intent. However, unlike Figure 1.1, this intent is more ambiguous as it could be that the bully is laughing at an incidental event.

Neither of these students self-identified as a bully or victim, however their speech bubbles indicate their understanding that bullying is intentional. When seeking students' understandings of bullying, one needs to be mindful of the influence of established educational programmes, school initiatives and anti-bullying policies, which are common features in many South Australian schools, as these may contribute to an understanding of bullying that closely aligns with that of researchers. However, unlike intent, power imbalance was easily identified in many young people's drawings.

FIGURE 1.1 Drawing by a fifteen-year-old boy

FIGURE 1.2 Drawing by a nine-year-old girl

Power

Power featured in students' drawings in a number of ways. Some, like this twelve-year-old girl in Figure 1.3, illustrated groups of bullies targeting one or more victims.

The speech bubble '*Ellie and Ellen are so fat and ugly!*' highlights another element of power: attractiveness. Using the words '*yeah*' suggests that there are some people in a group who actively support the bully, reinforcing Olweus' (1978, 1991) argument that there are different types of bullies and Salmivalli et al.'s (1996) theory on participant roles. Other students, like the nine-year-old girl in Figure 1.4, identified social status as a form of power.

While this nine-year-old girl depicts bullies as having a perceived higher social status than their victim, other students used positioning to illustrate power (see Figure 1.5).

Many, like this nine-year-old girl in Figure 1.6, used a difference in stature between the bully and victim, which has also been depicted in other pictures.

Ben, a bystander from Green's (2015) study, also supported the notion of power by describing bullying as:

> a kid like much bigger and not your age, like a bit older than you, like going up to you and starts swearing at you, like pushing you around and teasing you.

Like Ben, many four and five year olds describe bullying in terms of older or stronger versus younger or weaker (Mishna 2004). An age differential emerged in

FIGURE 1.3 Drawing by a twelve-year-old girl

FIGURE 1.4 Drawing by a nine-year-old girl

FIGURE 1.5 Drawing by a ten-year-old girl

FIGURE 1.6 Drawing by a nine-year-old girl

drawings as illustrated in Figure 1.7, where a thirteen-year-old girl used speech bubbles to demonstrate this imbalance of power and specifically allocated ages to each individual.

Similarly, in Figure 1.8, a seven-year-old boy depicted bullying by qualifying age variations, as well as bigger and smaller stature.

FIGURE 1.7 Drawing by a thirteen-year-old girl

FIGURE 1.8 Drawing by a seven-year-old boy

Power differentials, whether as groups, status, age, size or position, were evident in most students' drawings, highlighting that this element is central in their understandings of bullying.

Repetition

Although power was evident in the majority of student's drawings, repetition was harder to detect as most young people illustrated a single incident. However, one nine-year-old boy wrote the caption *'gets lots of rethinks but doesn't care'* implying that bullying is not an isolated incident and, for some, may be persistent (see Figure 1.9).

This same student drew three areas in the school where bullying occurred, possibly signifying a single bully targeting victims in a number of areas around the school. Alternatively, he could have been suggesting that there are a number of different bullies who bully in these three areas.

FIGURE 1.9 Drawing by a nine-year-old boy

The focus on repetition, however, became apparent in Green's (2015) study, which explored the voice of those either directly or indirectly involved in bullying. Leah, an eight-year-old girl who self-identified as a victim, described bullying by saying:

> *They [bullies] keep on doing something but they do something bad like fill your bag up with water and stuff … and I have to say doing something wrong lots and lots of times.*

For Leah, repetition was focal to her understanding of bullying, highlighting the relentless harassment she felt as a victim. In this same study, seven-year-old Rebecca, who self-identified as a bully, differentiated a fight from bullying by highlighting the repetitive nature of the latter:

> *A fight is when two people do wrestling sometimes. The other kind [bullying] is when you say something … and then you keep going on and on and on.*

Further highlighting the complexity of this social phenomenon, many young people included a range of methods employed by bullies in their drawings.

Indirect and direct bullying

Many girls illustrated indirect bullying in their drawings (Green 2015). This form of bullying, also referred to as social or relational bullying (Crick & Grotpeter 1995), is covert in nature. Often involving a third party, indirect bullying includes, but is not limited to, gossiping, spreading rumours, befriending others as a means of revenge and excluding members of the peer group (Björkqvist, Österman & Kaukiainen 1992; Lagerspetz, Björkqvist & Peltonen 1988). Social exclusion can start with simple facial gestures such as rolling of the eyes, tossing hair and turning away from a peer (Galen & Underwood 1997). Due to the covert nature of this form of bullying, the bully often remains unidentified and avoids reprimand and disapproval from others. Consequently, bullying is reinforced.

Figures 1.10 and 1.11 show groups of females teasing and excluding their victim. As a strategy to damage peer relationships, exclusion is more common among girls than boys (Björkqvist, Österman & Kaukiainen 1992). These drawings clearly depict social exclusion, which can involve a group or individual. The victim may be part of the same group as those who reject her, in which case the behaviour is more hurtful because the victim is being rejected by perceived friends. The impact of this behaviour is further exacerbated as female friendships are often intimate and dyadic, whereas males tend to interact with large groups of friends (Maccoby 1990). Therefore a female who is excluded by her friend(s) needs to establish new relationships to satisfy her need to belong. This is often difficult, as exclusion can involve other groups and, in some cases, an entire year level (Owens, Shute & Slee 2000), leaving the victim feeling isolated and alone.

FIGURE 1.10 Drawing by a nine-year-old girl

FIGURE 1.11 Drawing by an eleven-year-old girl

As highlighted earlier, this behaviour often goes undetected, increasing feelings of isolation. Thus, as will be illustrated in Leah's narrative in Chapter 2, indirect bullying has a particularly powerful and harmful impact on victims. To further understand this, one must consider Baumeister and Leary's (1995) argument that the need to belong is an innate 'fundamental human motivation' (p. 520), so much so that individuals endeavour to meet this need once basic requirements such as food and safety have been fulfilled (Baumeister & Leary 1995). On one hand, a sense of belonging is considered important to one's wellbeing as it provides a feeling of acceptance, attachment, support and positive identity, and can thus contribute to increased academic success. Rejection, on the other hand, can lead to anxiety, depression, grief, jealousy, isolation and loneliness (Baumeister & Leary 1995; Österman 2000). When considering these positive and negative dimensions of belonging, it is not surprising that social exclusion is seen as a powerful means of bullying and harming others, with the impact increasing if the victim perceives the rejecters as friends.

Although indirect bullying was prominent in students' drawings, there were some who included elements of direct physical bullying in their diagrams (see Figure 1.12).

As illustrated in Figure 1.13, other students included stealing as a means of bullying in their drawings.

Both indirect and direct bullying frequently occur in face-to-face settings, however young people also highlighted that with the emergence of technology, bullying can occur online.

FIGURE 1.12 Drawing by an eight-year-old boy

FIGURE 1.13 Drawing by a nine-year-old boy

Cyberbullying

What is cyberbullying? Understandings of cyberbullying are constantly evolving but commonly describe sending or posting harmful text or images using digital communication. Belsey (2011) suggests that it is

> the use of information and communication technologies such as e-mail, cell phone and pager text messages, instant messaging, defamatory personal Web sites, and defamatory online personal polling Web sites, to support deliberate, repeated, and hostile behaviour by an individual or group, that is intended to harm others.

Smith, Mahdavi, Carvalho, Fisher, Russell & Tippett (2008) combined these elements with features recognized in traditional bullying: 'an aggressive, intentional act carried out by a group or individual, using electronic forms of contact, repeatedly and over time against a victim who cannot easily defend him or herself' (p. 376). Unlike face-to-face bullying, cyberbullying typically occurs outside of school hours, is less frequent than face-to-face bullying, and yet has a larger impact on victims (Campbell, Spears, Slee, Butler & Kift 2012; Smith et al. 2008). It was therefore not surprising that students included this form of bullying in their drawings (see Figures 1.14 and 1.15).

FIGURE 1.14 Drawing by an eleven-year-old girl

FIGURE 1.15 Drawing by an eleven-year-old girl

A relationship between face-to-face and cyberbullying has been noted. Students who bully or are victimized face-to-face are also more likely to bully or be victimized online (Cross, Shaw, Hearn, Epstein, Monks, Lester & Thomas 2009; Li 2007). Movement from the offline environment to an online setting and back again has been noted, suggesting a cyclic relationship between both (Spears, Slee, Owens & Johnson 2009). This interaction between online and face-to-face schooling contexts is depicted in Figure 1.15. Chapter 9 will consider cyberbullying in more detail to further aid our understanding of persistent bullying and how it may traverse offline and online contexts.

Summary of young people's understandings

This chapter has explored young people's understandings of bullying, a necessary precursor to later discussions of persistent bullying. The use of drawings enabled young people to describe their understandings of bullying in a non-threatening way (Thomson 2008), resulting in many powerful illustrations. Students agreed that bullying is a negative behaviour that is repeated over time and carried out by a more powerful individual, supporting researchers' definitions (Farrington 1993; Farrington & Ttofi 2009; Olweus 1993). These young people not only demonstrated a sound understanding of what bullying is, they also identified some of the more complex issues such as repetition and its effect on the power balance in relationships, providing an insightful opening to our book.

Multiple perspectives on persistent bullying

Research in the area of bullying is extensive, yet there remains a need to hear the perspectives of those who are on the ground floor and have first-hand experience. Their lived experiences will aid understanding and add to our current knowledge in this area. Individual, family and school characteristics of those who bully and are bullied have been identified by researchers, and interventions aimed at reducing this behaviour in schools have been developed and employed around the world. Yet, despite this, interventions have achieved mixed results. A particular focus of this book is the identification of discrete bullying trajectories, one of which includes students who bully at consistently moderate or high levels (Pepler et al. 2008).

Persistent bullies are those students who continue bullying in spite of interventions and sanctions employed by schools. These students form the focus of *Multiple Perspectives in Persistent Bullying: Capturing and listening to young people's voices*. An understanding of their behaviour and why they may be resistant to change will be gained by accessing their lived experiences and those of their peers. Students who persistently bully challenge interventions by their relentless behaviour and have a negative impact on the schooling experiences and social and emotional wellbeing of their peers (Green 2015). When talking about persistent bullying, teachers in South Australian schools describe 'ongoing disruption, harassment, disruption to their learning' (female middle-years' teacher) and feeling 'stressed – angry

– despairing – [and] incompetent' (female junior primary teacher) (Green 2015). We suggest that these perceptions may be experienced by many teachers. As such, persistent bullying needs to be addressed in order to enhance the school experience of both students and teachers.

Many studies have focused on victims and bullies, yet considerably fewer have concentrated on those who persistently bully. Debra Pepler and colleagues (2008) identified four developmental trajectories that bullies may follow: starts low and increases; starts moderate and desists; starts moderate and remains moderate; and starts high and remains high. Elevated risks in the individual, parent, peer and relationship domains were identified as differentiating those who maintain moderate or high levels of bullying from those who were uninvolved in bullying (Pepler et al. 2008).

Multiple Perspectives in Persistent Bullying: Capturing and listening to young people's voices presents the voices of stakeholders who engage in, have been victimized by, or who have witnessed schoolyard bullying. In particular, these voices shed light on factors that reinforce persistent bullying, enabling us to understand why some bullies '*seem to get told off but they don't change – nothing happens*' (eight-year-old girl in Year 4) (Green 2015). The narratives of these young people provide new theoretical approaches to understanding this long-standing social phenomenon. This will inform school-based interventions aimed at improving the life outcomes and wellbeing of these students, their peers and the school community generally. In the following chapters, we consider the lived experiences of those impacted by bullying, starting with the narrative of Leah (a victim) in Chapter 2.

References

Baldry, A.C. & Winkel, F.W. (2003) Direct and vicarious victimization at school and at home as risk factors for suicide cognition among Italian adolescents. *Journal of Adolescence*, 26(6), pp. 703–716.

Baumeister, R.F. & Leary, M.R. (1995) The need to belong: Desire for interpersonal attachments as a fundamental human motivation. *Psychological Bulletin*, 117(3), pp. 497–529.

Belsey, B. (2011) *Cyberbullying.* Available from www.cyberbullying.ca/, accessed 24 November 2011.

Bernstein, J.Y. & Watson, M.W. (1997) Children who are targets of bullying. *Journal of Interpersonal Violence*, 12(4), pp. 483–499.

Björkqvist, K., Österman, K.F. & Kaukiainen, A. (1992) The development of direct and indirect strategies in males and females. In K. Björkqvist & P. Niemela (eds), *Of mice and women: Aspects of female aggression.* San Diego, CA: Academic Press, pp. 51–64.

Bond, L., Carlin, J.B., Thomas, L., Rubin, K. & Patton, G. (2001) Does bullying cause emotional problems? A prospective study of young teenagers. *British Medical Journal*, 323(7311), pp. 480–483.

Boulton, M.J. & Smith, P.K. (1994) Bully/victim problems in middle-school children: Stability, self-perceived competence, peer perceptions and peer acceptance. *British Journal of Developmental Psychology*, 12(3), pp. 315–329.

Campbell, M., Spears, B., Slee, P., Butler, D. & Kift, S. (2012) Victims' perceptions of traditional and cyberbullying, and the psychosocial correlates of their victimisation. *Emotional and Behavioural Difficulties*, 17(3–4), pp. 389–401.

Craig, W., Pepler, D. & Atlas, R. (2000) Observations of bullying in the playground and in the classroom. *School Psychology International*, 21(22), pp. 22–36.

Crick, N.R. & Grotpeter, J.K. (1995) Relational aggression, gender and social-psychological adjustment. *Child Development*, 66(3), pp. 710–722.

Cross, D., Shaw, T., Hearn, L., Epstein, M., Monks, H., Lester, L. & Thomas, L. (2009) *Australian covert bullying prevalence study (ACBPS)*. Perth: Edith Cowan University, Child Promotion Research Centre.

Farrington, D.P. (1993) Understanding and preventing bullying. In M. Tonry (ed), *Crime and justice: A review of research, vol. 17*. Chicago, IL: University of Chicago Press, pp. 381–458.

Farrington, D.P. & Ttofi, M.M. (2009) Reducing school bullying: evidence-based implications for policy. *Crime and Justice*, 38(1), pp. 281–345.

Galen, B.R. & Underwood, M.K. (1997) A developmental investigation of social aggression among children. *Developmental Psychology*, 33(4), pp. 589–600.

Green, D.M. (2015) An investigation of persistent bullying at school: Multiple perspectives of a complex social phenomenon. Doctoral dissertation, University of South Australia.

Hazler, R.J., Carney, J.V., Green, S., Powell, R. & Jolly, L.S. (1997) Areas of expert agreement on identification of school bullies and victims. *School Psychology International*, 18(1), pp. 5–14.

Hinduja, S. & Patchin, J.W. (2010) Bullying, cyberbullying, and suicide. *Archives of Suicide Research*, 14(3), pp. 206–221.

Kaltiala-Heino, R., Rimpelä, M., Marttunen, M., Rimpelä, A. & Rantanen, P. (2000) Bullying, depression, and suicidal ideation in Finnish adolescents: School survey. *British Medical Journal*, 319(7206), pp. 348–351.

Kim, Y.S. & Leventhal, B. (2008) Bullying and suicide: A review. *Journal of Adolescent Medicine and Health*, 20(2), pp. 133–154.

Kumpulainen, K., Räsänen, E. & Puura, K. (2001) Psychiatric disorders and the use of mental health services among children involved in bullying. *Aggressive Behavior*, 27(2), pp. 102–110.

Lagerspetz, K.M.J., Björkqvist, K. & Peltonen, T. (1988) Is indirect aggression typical of females? Gender differences in aggressiveness in 11- to 12-year-old children. *Aggressive Behavior*, 14(6), pp. 403–414.

Li, Q. (2007) New bottle but old wine: A research of cyberbullying in schools. *Computers in Human Behavior*, 23(4), pp. 1777–1791.

Maccoby, E.E. (1990) Gender and relationships: A developmental account. *American Psychologist*, 36(6), pp. 513–520.

Mishna, F. (2004) A qualitative study of bullying from multiple perspectives. *Children & Schools*, 26(4), pp. 234–247.

Olweus, D. (1978) *Aggression in the schools: Bullies and whipping boys*. Washington, DC: Hemisphere.

Olweus, D. (1991) Victimization among school children. In R. Baenninger (ed), *Targets of violence and aggression*. Philadelphia, PA: Temple University, pp. 45–102.

Olweus, D. (1993) *Bullying at school: What we know and what we can do*. Oxford: Blackwell.

Olweus, D. (1994) Bullying at school: Long-term outcomes for the victims and an effective school-based intervention program. In L.R. Huesmann (ed), *Aggressive behaviour: Current perspectives*. New York, NY: Plenum Press, pp. 97–130.

Olweus, D. (1995) Bullying or peer abuse at school: Facts and intervention. *Journal of the American Psychological Society*, 4(6), pp. 196–200.

Olweus, D. (1996) Bully/victim problems in school. *Prospects*, 26(2), pp. 331–359.

Österman, K.F. (2000) Students' need for belonging in the school community. *Review of Educational Research*, 70(3), pp. 323–367.

Owens, L., Shute, R. & Slee, P. (2000) 'Guess what I just heard!': Indirect aggression among teenage girls in Australia. *Aggressive Behavior*, 26(1), pp. 67–83.

Pepler, D.J. (2006) Bullying interventions: A binocular perspective. *Canadian Journal of Child Adolescent Psychiatry*, 15(1), pp. 16–20.

Pepler, D.J., Jiang, D., Craig, W.M. & Connolly, J. (2008) Developmental trajectories of bullying and associated factors. *Child Development*, 79(2), pp. 325–338.

Salmivalli, C. (2010) Bullying and the peer group: A review. *Aggression and Violent Behavior*, 15(2), pp. 112–120.

Salmivalli, C., Lagerspetz, K.M.J., Björkqvist, K., Österman, K. & Kaukiainen, A. (1996) Bullying as a group process: Participant roles and their relations to social status within the group. *Aggressive Behavior*, 22(1), pp. 1–15.

Sampson, R. (2002) Bullying in schools. Problem-oriented guides for police series (no. 12). Available from www.cops.usdoj.gov, accessed 3 January 2012.

Schwartz, D., Dodge, K.A. & Coie, J.D. (1993) The emergence of chronic peer victimization in boys' play groups. *Child Development*, 64(6), pp. 1755–1772.

Sentse, M., Scholte, R., Salmivalli, C. & Voeten, M. (2007) Person-group dissimilarity in involvement in bullying and its relation with social status. *Journal of Abnormal Child Psychology*, 35(6), pp. 1009–1019.

Smith, P., Madsen, K. & Moody, J. (1999) What causes the age decline in reports of being bullied at school? Towards a developmental analysis of risks of being bullied. *Educational Research*, 41(3), pp. 267–285.

Smith, P.K., Cowie, H., Olafsson, R.F. & Liefooghe, A.P.D. (2002) Definitions of bullying: A comparison of terms used, and age and gender differences, in a fourteen-country international comparison. *Child Development*, 73(4), pp. 1119–1133.

Smith, P.K., Mahdavi, J., Carvalho, M., Fisher, S., Russell, S. & Tippett, N. (2008) Cyberbullying: Its nature and impact in secondary school pupils. *Journal of Child Psychology & Psychiatry*, 49(4), pp. 376–385.

Spears, B., Johnson, B., Scrimgeour, M., Geer, R., Price, D. & Green, D.M. (2009/2010) *Cyber bystanders: The role of the bystander in cyberspace and cyberbullying in an Australian context*. University of South Australia, Divisional Research Performance Fund.

Spears, B., Slee, P., Owens, L. & Johnson, B. (2009) Behind the scenes and screens: Insights into the human dimension of covert and cyberbullying. *Journal of Psyhology*, 217(4), pp. 189–196.

Thomson, P. (2008) Children and young people: Voices in visual research. In P. Thomson (ed), *Doing visual research with children and young people*. New York, NY: Routledge, pp. 1–19.

PART II

The voices of those who are victimized

2

LEAH: VICTIM

I try and ignore it but if it's really getting in my thing then I actually do kind of …
I tell mum and I tell the teachers and I try and stay right away from them if I possibly
can … I keep my hat down [so the bully cannot see me] and we also have a 'stop
I don't like it' sign in our school.

(Leah, eight years old)

Tragically, bullying has a negative impact on everyone, particularly those who are
targeted by the behaviour. This chapter begins to expose the multiple perspectives
of persistent bullying by hearing the experiences of those who have been targets
of this behaviour. Being the recipient of persistent victimization has been found
to negatively affect educational achievement, school attendance, as well as future
aspirations (Beale 2001; Kowalski, Limber & Agatston 2008). Over time, victims
may begin to view themselves in a negative light, causing internalizing problems
such as anxiety, depression and eating disorders (Bond, Carlin, Thomas, Rubin &
Patton 2001). In extreme cases, victims seek retribution against their bully (Carney
& Merrell 2001) while others may attempt suicide (Baldry & Winkel 2003). Despite
the suffering experienced by victims, and the consistent call for young people to
report bullying, many observe a code of silence, preferring not to report incidents
(Smith & Shu 2000). This can be due to a number of reasons including: having little
faith in adult responses; being concerned about how others might perceive them;
fearing retaliation; feeling shame or weakness; fearing that others will not believe
them; being concerned about worrying their parents or others; fearing the situation may get worse; or being concerned about being called a 'snitch' or 'dobber'
(Sampson 2002). Compounding this is the concern that disclosures are limited to
extreme cases or where a student has experienced persistent bullying, leaving minor,
less frequent incidents unreported (Unnever 2005). To further understand decisions
regarding whether or not to report bullying, Part II focuses on giving voice to those

who have been victimized. We begin by introducing 'Leah', an eight-year-old girl who self-identified as being victimized by same-age and older peers.

Leah is in Year 3 at school. When asked to describe herself, Leah proudly states that she is a *'nice person that would help out'*. Leah's mum describes her as:

> *my chatterbox, she always has an opinion and knows everything. As Leah is my baby and her father died when I was pregnant with her, so I have been over supportive of everything she wants to do. Therefore Leah tends to come across as confident, assertive but I know she is unsure of her abilities underneath ... [she is] unsettled and sometimes aggressive and emotional.*

Teachers also see Leah in a positive light describing her as *'a good student but she doesn't have friends'*. Leah agrees that, despite a strong desire to belong and be accepted, she experiences extreme difficulties gaining and maintaining friendships. Although she describes feeling happy at school, Leah would like to have friends that accept and regularly include her.

Family and peer relationships

Leah's father passed away before she was born, leaving her, her mum and her older sister. She is part of a close-knit, large, extended family and feels closest to her mum, who she believes will always be able to protect her. Leah does not share this same closeness with her sister, which she regrets. Leah's family decided to move from Queensland to Adelaide and Leah found it difficult to leave her school friends behind. At the time of the interview, Leah had been at her new school in Adelaide for approximately six months.

Transitions are challenging for most students, and starting a new school is often met with excitement and anxiety. Leah described her first days at her new school as difficult because *'it's a big thing when it's your first day, it's kind of, you can't really find anything, it's hard'*. This was accentuated by her difficulties with feeling accepted and gaining friendships, which will be discussed later in this chapter. Referring to the move from Queensland to South Australia Leah said, *'it was quite hard because ... no one wanted to play with me today you really wanted to be up there so I'd have someone to play with'*. Leah still misses her Queensland friends and looks forward to holidays when she can visit and spend time with them.

Leah chose not to talk specifically about her current friends but instead waited to be asked. She recalled that *'I had a couple of problems 'cause sometimes people didn't want to play with me so I'd get upset'*. Leah longed for a close friend *'who plays with you a lot ... doesn't really matter if she's playing with another friend she can still play ... and you know invite you over to her house maybe birthdays as well'*. For Leah, this demonstrated their acceptance and loyalty towards her. Outside of school Leah had a couple of friends who are older than her. Although she describes these girls as friends, at school they bully her, refuse to play with her and '*try to push me out*'. This further compounded Leah's socialization difficulties and sense of isolation.

In her new school Leah reports spending many break times alone with no one to play with. To address this, Leah often spends recess and lunch breaks helping and interacting with her teachers as opposed to playing with peers. This is not uncommon as poor peer relationships see victims, like Leah, relating better to adults, which further alienates them from their peer group (Olweus 1993).

A consistent message through Leah's description of her experiences was her strong desire to belong and have friends. She did anything that would help her to fulfil these needs. In fact, belonging has a high priority in society, being positioned second behind the human need for food and shelter (Baumeister & Leary 1995; Österman 2000). To help Leah fit in at school, her teacher would often intervene: '*Okay can everyone sit down because I want to have a talk about something*' and she'd say '*Can people include and talk to Leah?*' Although well-meaning, this unfortunately publicly highlighted Leah's lack of friends and sense of belonging, making her feel even more isolated and reducing her status among her peers. Leah may have been more effectively supported if the teacher implemented social skills training for the entire class rather than making direct public reference to Leah.

Victims of bullying, such as Leah, have been found to be more widely disliked by their peers and they also identify having more enemies than others in their peer group (Abecassis, Hartup, Haselager, Scholte & Van Lieshout 2002; Card & Hodges 2007). Although Leah is not actively disliked by her peers, she appears to lack the necessary social and adjustment skills to gain and maintain friends. Consequently, like many victims, she describes feelings of loneliness (Nansel, Overpeck, Pilla, Ruan, Simons-Morton & Scheidt 2001). This means that she experiences difficulty identifying with a network of friends and therefore experiences a lower perceived social identity than her peers, placing her at risk of further victimization (Rodkin & Hodges 2003; Cassidy 2009).

Despite feelings of rejection and isolation, Leah is to be commended on her persistent efforts to make friends. She demonstrates a strong sense of agency and believes that it is her responsibility to '*get more friends so I've got someone too that I can stick with and play with*'. This tenacious attitude is admirable and contributes to her resilience. However, friends act as a buffer against future victimization; therefore it is concerning that Leah is experiencing such peer relationship difficulties. Emphasizing the importance of relationships, Pepler (2006) suggests that bullying should be seen as a relationship problem.

Leah's understandings and experiences of bullying and persistent bullying

For Leah, bullying is a repetitive act towards another person or people:

> *They [bullies] keep on doing something but they do something bad like fill your bag up with water and stuff … and I have to say doing something wrong lots and lots of times.*

She identifies any action that causes harm as bullying. Leah's definition is consistent with other children her age, highlighting the nature of children's developing understanding of bullying (Monks & Smith 2006; Cheng, Chen, Ho & Cheng 2011). She recognizes both direct and indirect forms of bullying and explains that social exclusion is bullying because '*it makes someone feel hurt*'. Leah further explains that both boys and girls bully however '*it's mostly boys*'; a view that is consistent with the literature (Jolliffe & Farrington 2006; Olweus 1978; Rigby & Slee 2008). In her eyes, bullying is not restricted to children as '*adults still can bully each other … it goes around … your mum or your dad or anyone that you know*'. Leah also views bullying as '*something that normally happens to everyone, most everyone would have a time in their life of getting bullied*'. This view is concerning as it suggests an acceptance that may affect her decision to disclose in the future.

Initially, Leah identified similar physical characteristics for bullies and victims, yet when asked explicitly to describe each, she articulated that bullies '*try and look big and tough*' while victims '*probably have bruises all over them*'. She further explained that '*bullies are quite big and the ones that they are trying to pick on are smaller than their ages so they can try and get them a bit better*'. Leah's description mirrors earlier research in the area of children's perceptions of bullying (Olweus 1993). She clearly identifies a power imbalance, something that was consistent with the views of victims in Cheng et al.'s (2011) study.

Leah understands direct physical bullying; however, she does not demonstrate the same level of understanding or recognition of the more discreet, indirect forms of bullying. This is interesting as Leah herself describes incidents of relational bullying. Although she describes bullying as repeatedly '*doing something bad*' she also believes that it is her responsibility '*to try and get more friends so I've got someone that I can stick with and play with*'. This possibly explains why she does not recognize exclusion as an act of bullying. Leah's experiences of bullying have influenced her understandings of it, therefore insights into these experiences and her perceptions of persistent bullying are important.

When talking about her own experiences of being bullied, Leah's body language changes. She folds her arms and regularly makes fists with her hands. Leah speaks of incidents of relational and indirect bullying where she is often rejected by a group of her peers.

> *They just don't want to play with me and they kind of go 'No you're not playing with me'. They can go, you know, 'if I keep on doing that to [Leah] then she'll just feel more left out'.*

Like Leah, victims of relational bullying often believe that acts such as exclusion are normal (Mishna 2004). This raises the question of why victims don't consider these indirect acts as bullying when there have been educational initiatives employed by schools globally and extensive media coverage which explicitly states the contrary. It would seem that many factors influence victims' understandings. First, social exclusion and peer rejection are often considered to be a consequence of non-conformity to social norms, therefore victims may feel responsible for what is happening to them (Cranham & Carroll 2003; Kless 1992). Second, relational bullying is generally considered less serious and harmful than other more direct forms of bullying, therefore the damage is often overlooked (Batsche & Knoff 1994; Craig, Henderson & Murphy 2000). Teachers are also less likely to intervene when relational bullying is reported (Owens, Shute & Slee 2000), something that students are aware of. Students often believe that teachers will not consider exclusion to be serious and, even if they do, they may still ignore it (Thomson & Gunter 2008). Therefore, if students like Leah believe that relational bullying is not serious and nothing will happen if they disclose, they will be less likely to report incidents in the future and more likely to see the behaviour as normal (Landau, Milich, Harris & Larson 2001). Third, some parents tell their children to merely ignore what is happening or avoid situations where relational bullying may occur (Mishna 2004). This parental advice can confirm a child's belief that such acts are not serious and, instead of reporting, they need to be proactive in addressing the situation; something that was evident in Leah's approach. It is therefore not uncommon for victims to believe that they need to manage the problem on their own as opposed to seeking the support of an adult (Clarke & Kiselica 1997; Smith & Myron-Wilson 1998). In Leah's case, she blames herself, believing that the onus is on her '*to try and get more friends*'. She does not want those who bully her to be reprimanded, believing it will provide only temporary relief. Instead, she reasons that it is up to her to develop friendships, further demonstrating her ability to take responsibility for things that occur in her life. She explains that she needs to '*try and move away and try and get other friends because if they keep on doing it then I've got probably no one*'. Leah demonstrates maturity, believing that it is her responsibility to foster new friendships as opposed to punishing those who bully her and suggests that other victims should '*stay away from that area … and make sure that your face is half covered … most covered because … you know have your hat down a bit because then you know they can't really see that it's you*'.

Leah describes persistent bullies as '*quite big and strong*' and '*scared of something, which you need to kind of figure out*'. She proposes that students who persistently bully may lack friends and engage in bullying to meet their need to belong and increase their status among peers. Leah also believes that bullying enables them to provide fun for themselves and those around them, thus increasing their acceptance and popularity:

> *It makes them feel good because, you know, they can have … a really good laugh at someone because, you know, they hurt someone and got 'em down because they're hurting the person and they go … 'I'm popular now and I'm going to tell my friends that I got someone down … and I'm popular and … I've got heaps of friends. I can tell them and have a really big laugh and joke about the person'.*

According to Leah, persistent bullies have '*learned it* [bullying]*; they may have seen someone hurting another person they've probably copied that … it's on the roads and …*

sometimes at home you can look out the window and you can find people hurt each other'. She believes that schools should

> *give them [persistent bullies] another chance if they do it again … try to, say, have a big talk about how bad is bullying and then try and say … 'if I was the bully and you were the person getting hurt how would you feel about it?'*

If this fails, Leah believes that expulsion is the only option. Demonstrating an ability to empathize with persistent bullies, Leah further believes that teachers need to help by investigating what is happening in their lives. Despite this, when presented with the hypothetical scenario of a child being knocked over in the tuckshop line by someone known to be a bully, Leah immediately identified the act as intentional.

Having gained insights into Leah's understandings and perceptions of bullying and persistent bullying, it is important to identify what life factors have placed her at risk of being bullied.

Risk factors and protective mechanisms

A secure attachment to a caregiver provides a safe base to explore the world and can act as a buffer to bullying, however this did not appear to be the case for Leah. Her family provided support during difficult times and a safe base from which to learn, experiment and develop. In particular, Leah described a secure attachment to her mother, however, this did not appear to protect her from being victimized, which may suggest that more than one secure relationship is needed. Nevertheless it provided her with the confidence to disclose to her mother and teacher what was happening and to take action to improve her situation. The importance of secure attachments, particularly with caregivers, cannot be understated, as these early bonds shape internal representations of the environment, influencing future social experiences (Thompson & Raikes 2003). The literature highlights that those who experience an insecure attachment may develop a negative bias that affects their future social interactions, making them more likely to bully or be bullied (Walden & Beran 2010). While recognizing that a secure attachment to her mother has in some ways helped Leah, a lack of attachment to a father figure apparently placed her at risk of being victimized. Increasing Leah's risk was a mother, who in her own words, was *'oversupportive and overprotective'* (Bowers, Smith & Binney 1994; Olweus 1993; Orpinas & Horne 2006). In Leah's case, we suggest that a multi-layering of risk factors is evident.

Positive relationships with significant adults, and particularly teachers, can provide a sense of belonging that acts as a buffer for students, like Leah, who are experiencing bullying and peer rejection (Green, Oswald & Spears 2007; Österman 2000). Teachers are socialization agents, with student–teacher relationships having a powerful influence on children's social development (Davis 2003). Positive relationships with teachers can help develop students' sense of belonging (Goodenow

1993; Österman 2000) and social identity. This was important to Leah, who had transitioned from interstate and was struggling to make friends. Leah's teachers were aware of the peer relationship difficulties she was experiencing and, on many occasions, attempted to address this with the class but to no avail. Like many victims, Leah often spent break times helping her teachers in an attempt to fulfil her sense of belonging. Unfortunately, this appeared to further alienate her from her peer group and did not help her to learn the social skills needed to gain and maintain friendships. This resulted in Leah often feeling different from her peers and isolated at school.

Leah's difficulty in gaining and maintaining friendships is concerning as these relationships can act as a buffer against bullying. Whether a child is victimized or not is largely determined by the quantity and quality of their friendships (Rodkin & Hodges 2003), making it important for a child to establish positive dyadic or group relationships. Such friendships are clearly missing in Leah's life at the moment. Sadly, when a child has no reciprocal best friend they are more likely to be victimized than peers who have a best friend (Rodkin & Hodges 2003). This places Leah at a greater risk of being bullied.

Leah's peers will often play with her on one day and reject her the next, leaving her to find someone else '*who is playing with no one*'. When this happens, she feels sad and isolated. Friendships are important to Leah and she spoke about them constantly. Leah would like a friend who '*invites you over to her house maybe birthdays as well*', something that is normal for many young people. She expresses a need to belong and be accepted. Difficult peer relationships, such as those experienced by Leah, unfortunately increase her risk of being victimized. She has few or no friends and her peers are unable or unwilling to provide protection when she is being bullied (Hodges & Perry 1996). However, should Leah develop secure friendships, this could act as a buffer against future victimization (Boulton, Trueman, Chau, Whitehand & Amatya 1999; Hodges, Boivin, Vitaro & Bukowski 1999; Hodges, Malone & Perry 1997; Orpinas & Horne 2006). To do this, she needs to develop the necessary social skills to gain and maintain friendships.

Through Leah's own narrative she identifies that she lacks the necessary social skills to make and maintain strong friendships (e.g. good conflict management strategies, group entry skills), possibly contributing to her victimization (Eisenberg, Fabes & Spinrad 2006; Sroufe & Fleeson 1988). We suggest that relationships provide a reciprocal training ground for learning social skills in which friends learn from each other. Leah's challenges in employing the necessary social skills to gain and maintain friendships suggest that she did not appear to have the training ground to learn these crucial skills. Without these skills, the likelihood of persistent rejection and victimization is increased (Dodge et al. 2003; Ladd 1999). As such, we suggest that foundational experiences in social skill development, family experiences, and environmental transitions may have acted as critical turning points in Leah's trajectory.

Chapter summary

Leah has been excluded by her peers. While she sees exclusion as a way of compelling her to develop friendships, it has negatively affected her school experience. As expressed through her own voice, Leah highlighted the importance of needing to belong and be accepted. This was further illustrated in the qualities she values in friends: acceptance and loyalty. Leah does not see exclusion as a form of bullying, believing she is to blame as she needs to learn to make new friends. Often her teacher speaks to the entire class about the importance of accepting others, specifically mentioning Leah, which helps for a short time. Although well-meaning, this approach draws attention to Leah's lack of belonging, subsequently reducing her status among her peers and increasing her risk of future victimization.

When talking about persistent bullying, Leah demonstrates empathy towards those who bully. She believes that a need to belong – something that she identifies with – actually motivates and reinforces persistent bullying. Explicitly teaching persistent bullies about the effect of their behaviour was among Leah's suggestions to reduce the behaviour in schools. Of note, in Leah's eyes school incidents were deemed to be intentional if the person committing an act was a known bully (Dodge 1980; Ladd 1999).

Although Leah is bullied both inside and outside of school she never retaliates *'because I'm just going to say if I hurt them back then they'll just go for longer and longer and then it will just get worse'*. Instead, she demonstrates self-regulation and works towards making friends. Leah seeks support from teachers and others in developing friendships which potentially may buffer her against victimization and provide a sense of belonging.

Leah's experience is but one of many victim perspectives which have dominated the field, yet bullying persists with detrimental outcomes. Leah is eight years old and has been bullied since starting school three years ago. We challenge the reader to contemplate what Leah's life would be like if she continues to be bullied throughout her thirteen years of schooling? While Leah is resilient and takes a degree of responsibility, we suggest that her peers, teachers, family and broader educational community also need to take responsibility in order to provide a turning point to circumvent further bullying. In returning to the definition presented in Chapter 1, persistent bullies are those students who continue to bully in spite of interventions and sanctions. Given Leah has experienced bullying for all of her initial schooling years, the question needs to be asked at what point does this become persistent victimization? Chapter 3 extends this discussion by exploring the voice of victims and sharing the lived experiences of Brooke, who self-identifies as being persistently victimized throughout her entire school life.

References

Abecassis, M., Hartup, W.W., Haselager, G.J.T., Scholte, R.H.J. & Van Lieshout, C.F.M. (2002) Mutual antipathies and their significance in middle childhood and adolescence. *Child Development*, 73(5), pp. 1543–1556.

Baldry, A.C. & Winkel, F.W. (2003) Direct and vicarious victimization at school and at home as risk factors for suicide cognition among Italian adolescents. *Journal of Adolescence*, 26(6), pp. 703–716.

Batsche, G.M. & Knoff, H.M. (1994) Bullies and their victims: Understanding a pervasive problem in the schools. *School Psychology Review*, 23(2), pp. 165–175.

Baumeister, R.F. & Leary, M.R. (1995) The need to belong: Desire for interpersonal attachments as a fundamental human motivation. *Psychological Bulletin*, 117(3), pp. 497–529.

Beale, A.V. (2001) Bullybusters: Using drama to empower students to take a stand against bullying behavior. *Professional School Counseling*, 4(4), pp. 300–306.

Bond, L., Carlin, J.B., Thomas, L., Rubin, K. & Patton, G. (2001) Does bullying cause emotional problems? A prospective study of young teenagers. *British Medical Journal*, 323(7311), pp. 480–483.

Boulton, M.J., Trueman, M., Chau, C., Whitehand, C. & Amatya, K. (1999) Concurrent and longitudinal links between friendship and peer victimization: Implications for befriending interventions. *Journal of Adolescence*, 22(4), pp. 461–466.

Bowers, L., Smith, P.K. & Binney, V. (1994) Perceived family relationships of bullies, victims and bully/victims in middle childhood. *Journal of Social and Personal Relationships*, 11(2), pp. 215–232.

Card, N.A. & Hodges, E.V.E. (2007) Victimization within mutually antipathetic peer relationships. *Social Development*, 16(3), pp. 479–496.

Carney, A.G. & Merrell, K.W. (2001) Bullying in schools: Perspectives on understanding and preventing an international problem. *School Psychology International*, 22(3), pp. 364–382.

Cassidy, T. (2009) Bullying and victimisation in school children: The role of social identity, problem-solving style, and family and school context. *Social Psychology of Education*, 12(1), pp. 63–76.

Cheng, Y.-Y., Chen, L.-M., Ho, H.-C. & Cheng, C.-L. (2011) Definitions of school bullying in Taiwan: A comparison of multiple perspectives. *School Psychology International*, 32(3), pp. 227–243.

Clarke, E.A. & Kiselica, M.S. (1997) A systemic counseling approach to the problem of bullying. *Elementary School Guidance & Counseling*, 31(4), pp. 310–325.

Craig, W.M., Henderson, K. & Murphy, J.G. (2000) Prospective teachers' attitudes toward bullying and victimization. *School Psychology International*, 21(1), pp. 5–21.

Cranham, J. & Carroll, A. (2003) Dynamics within the bully/victim paradigm: A qualitative analysis. *Educational Psychology in Practice*, 19(2), pp. 113–132.

Davis, H.A. (2003) Conceptualizing the role and influence of student–teacher relationships on children's social and cognitive development. *Educational Psychologist*, 38(4), pp. 207–234.

Dodge, K.A. (1980) Social cognition and children's aggressive behavior. *Child Development*, 51(1), pp. 162–170.

Dodge, K.A., Lansford, J.E., Burks, V.S., Bates, J.E., Pettit, G.S., Fontaine, R. & Price, J.M. (2003) Peer rejection and social information-processing factors in the development of aggressive behavior problems in children. *Child Development*, 74(2), pp. 374–393.

Eisenberg, N., Fabes, R. & Spinrad, T.L. (2006) Prosocial behavior. In N. Eisenberg, W. Damon & R. Lerner (eds), *Handbook of child psychology: Social, emotional and personality development, 6th edn, vol. 3*. New York, NY: Wiley, pp. 646–718.

Goodenow, C. (1993) The psychological sense of school membership among adolescents: Scale development and educational correlates. *Psychology in the Schools*, 30(1), pp. 79–90.

Green, D.M., Oswald, M. & Spears, B. (2007) Teachers' (mis)understandings of resilience. *International Education Journal*, 8(2), pp. 133–144.

Hodges, E.V.E. & Perry, D.G. (1996) Victims of peer abuse: An overview. *Reclaiming Children and Youth: The Journal of Emotional and Behavioral Problems*, 5(1), pp. 23–28.

Hodges, E.V.E., Boivin, M., Vitaro, F. & Bukowski, W.M. (1999) The power of friendship: Protection against an escalating cycle of peer victimization. *Developmental Psychology*, 35(1), pp. 94–101.

Hodges, E.V.E., Malone, M.J. & Perry, D.G. (1997) Individual risk and social risk as interacting determinants of victimization in the peer group. *Developmental Psychology*, 33(6), pp. 1032–1039.

Jolliffe, D. & Farrington, D.P. (2006) Examining the relationship between low empathy and bullying. *Aggressive Behavior*, 32(6), pp. 540–550.

Kless, S.J. (1992) The attainment of peer status: Gender and power relationships in the elementary school. *Sociological Studies of Child Development*, 5, pp. 115–148.

Kowalski, R., Limber, S. & Agatston, P. (2008) *Cyber bullying*. Malden, MA: Blackwell Publishing.

Ladd, G.W. (1999) Peer relationships and social competence during early and middle childhood. *Annual Review of Psychology*, 50(1), pp. 333–359.

Landau, S., Milich, R., Harris, M.J. & Larson, S.E. (2001) 'You really don't know how much it hurts:' Children's and preservice teachers' reactions to childhood teasing. *School Psychology Review*, 30(3), pp. 329–343.

Mishna, F. (2004) A qualitative study of bullying from multiple perspectives. *Children & Schools*, 26(4), pp. 234–247.

Monks, C.P. & Smith, P.K. (2006) Definitions of bullying: Age differences in understanding of the term, and the role of experience. *British Journal of Developmental Psychology*, 24(4), pp. 801–821.

Nansel, T.R., Overpeck, M., Pilla, R.S., Ruan, W.J., Simons-Morton, B. & Scheidt, P. (2001) Bullying behaviors among US youth: Prevalence and association with psychosocial adjustment. *JAMA: Journal of the American Medical Association*, 285(16), pp. 2094–2100.

Olweus, D. (1978) *Aggression in the schools: Bullies and whipping boys*. Washington, DC: Hemisphere.

Olweus, D. (1993) *Bullying at school: What we know and what we can do*. Oxford: Blackwell.

Orpinas, P. & Horne, A.M. (2006) *Bullying prevention: Creating a positive school climate and developing social competence*. Washington, DC: American Psychological Association.

Österman, K.F. (2000) Students' need for belonging in the school community. *Review of Educational Research*, 70(3), pp. 323–367.

Owens, L., Shute, R. & Slee, P. (2000) 'Guess what I just heard!': Indirect aggression among teenage girls in Australia. *Aggressive Behavior*, 26(1), pp. 67–83.

Pepler, D.J. (2006) Bullying interventions: A binocular perspective. *Canadian Journal of Child Adolescent Psychiatry*, 15(1), pp. 16–20.

Rigby, K. & Slee, P. (2008) Interventions to reduce bullying. *International Journal of Adolescent Medicine and Health*, 20(2), pp. 165–183.

Rodkin, P.C. & Hodges, E.V.E. (2003) Bullies and victims in the peer ecology: Four questions for psychologists and school professionals. *School Psychology Review*, 32(3), pp. 384–400.

Sampson, R. (2002) Bullying in schools. Problem-oriented guides for police series (no. 12). Available from www.cops.usdoj.gov, accessed 3 January 2012.

Smith, P.K. & Myron-Wilson, R. (1998) Parenting and school bullying. *Clinical Child Psychology and Psychiatry*, 3(3), pp. 405–417.

Smith, P.K. & Shu, S. (2000) What good schools can do about bullying: Findings from a survey in English schools after a decade of research and action. *Childhood*, 7(2), pp. 193–212.

Sroufe, L.A. & Fleeson, J. (1988) The coherence of family relationships. In R. Hinde & J. Stevenson-Hinde (eds), *Relationships within families: Mutual influences*. Oxford, Oxford University Press, pp. 27–47.

Thompson, R.A. & Raikes, H.A. (2003) Toward the next quarter-century: Conceptual and methodological challenges for attachment theory. *Development and Psychopathology*, 15(3), pp. 691–718.

Thomson, P. & Gunter, H. (2008) Researching bullying with students: A lens on everyday life in an 'innovative school'. *International Journal of Inclusive Education*, 12(2), pp. 185–200.

Unnever, J.D. (2005) Bullies, aggressive victims, and victims: Are they distinct groups? *Aggressive Behavior*, 31(2), pp. 153–171.

Walden, L.M. & Beran, T.N. (2010) Attachment quality and bullying behavior in school-aged youth. *Canadian Journal of School Psychology*, 25(1), pp. 5–18.

3

BROOKE: PERSISTENTLY VICTIMIZED

She didn't care ... she was just rocking up, it looked like to intimidate me ... she was getting a thrill out of seeing me scared ... she was always walking around the school ... I don't know what she was doing ... just the looks ... it's funny how much power a look can have and how scary it can feel.

(Brooke, 23 years old)

The intimidation and fear that 'Brooke' feels at the hands of a persistent bully is a common theme which continues to haunt many adults long after their compulsory schooling years. In Chapter 2 we introduced our discussion of victimization by outlining the effects of bullying on victims and giving voice to Leah, an eight-year-old girl who had experienced bullying at school. This chapter extends the discussion by introducing Brooke, a 23 year old who is in her final year of a Bachelor of Education. Brooke's story provides insights into the life of someone who was persistently victimized throughout her school years.

Family and peer relationships

During her school life Brooke lived in a small South Australian country town with her mum, dad and younger brother. As a result of her father's self-disclosed homosexuality, her parents separated when Brooke was in primary school. This was a difficult time for Brooke as she was *'seen as different'* and felt alienated from her peers. Brooke's younger brother was also involved in a near-fatal car accident, resulting in the family spending considerable time at an Adelaide hospital, which further alienated Brooke from her peers. She cried as she recollected this difficult time in her life. Part of her brother's rehabilitation involved learning to walk and talk again and Brooke played an active role in supporting and caring for him. Her parents, who were preoccupied with their pending divorce, left most of their son's care to nine-year-old Brooke. Family court orders ensured that Brooke maintained contact with her father until she was 13. At school, Brooke was teased and bullied about her parent's separation and more particularly her dad's sexuality; therefore she further alienated herself from him. She explains that she was torn because she still loved her dad but didn't want to be near him because of the pain he was causing her. Growing up, Brooke was not close to either parent, however she was – and still is – very close to her brother: *'My brother, it was always my brother'*. Relationships are important to Brooke, whether they be with teachers, friends or other adults. In high school, Brooke began to act promiscuously to gain a sense of belonging and acceptance from her peers. Despite feeling lonely among peers, she fondly recalls teachers who spent additional time outside of school helping her.

Friendships serve many functions and are considered a quintessential 'basic feature of human life from early childhood to old age' (Bukowski, Motzoi & Meyer 2009, p. 217). According to Asher and Parker (1989), friendships provide support, self-validation, emotional security, intimacy, affection, guidance, acceptance, alliance, companionship, stimulation, and opportunities to develop social competence. The need to belong is vital and, if not met, may lead to anti-social behaviours such as bullying (Baumeister & Leary 1995). For Brooke, despite having a best friend throughout school, she often felt that she did not belong. Brooke and her closest friend attended all the same parties, worked part-time in the same business and were always seen together. They never argued or fought and Brooke cherished her relationship with this girl. Despite this friendship, Brooke was continually victimized, which signaled that her closest friend lacked the confidence and/or skills to intervene and, unfortunately, at times supported the bully for fear of being attacked herself (Pellegrini, Bartini & Brooks 1999; Salmivalli, Huttunen & Lagerspetz 1997).

Going to university marked a change in Brooke's friendships as she no longer had a single best friend but instead held very close relationships with a small group of girls. These girls had previously attended the same high school as Brooke and, as they were all from the country, they supported each other in their transition to the city. As a result of this support, they developed close friendships. Brooke lacked the energy to form relationships with new people, which was a direct result of her persistent victimization. Therefore this group of friends provided a sense of belonging without Brooke needing to engage with new peers.

Brooke's perspectives on bullying, and particularly on persistent bullying, help us to understand this phenomenon from a victim's point of view and will be contrasted in Chapter 6 when we consider the perspective of John, a persistent bully.

Brooke's understandings and experiences of bullying and persistent bullying

Brooke describes bullying as *'hurtful and demeaning to the person that you are targeting'*, clearly acknowledging an intent to harm. She differentiates bullying from a fight because of its repetitive nature: '*bullying is like a continuous fight, it's a struggle, you don't know when it's going to end*'. Insight into the meaning and impact of bullying can be gained through Brooke's description of victims:

> *Different; I think that's just it … if you are different in any way, if you don't fit in, if you haven't got all the latest things or just don't know about whatever is going on in the … maybe not the world when you're younger but … if you don't watch this TV program or something like that then you're easily targeted.*

Brooke's understandings of bullying are underpinned by her own experiences, therefore her perceptions on persistent bullying are revealing.

> *I remember being on the ground just like praying that it would stop and I'm, there was so many people around watching … I felt so sore, I felt so bruised and I just remember saying to God 'Just take it away just take away all of this pain'.*

Brooke was first victimized at the age of nine; it got worse once she entered high school, and continued throughout her entire school life. For her, a number of life experiences differentiated her from her peers and resulted in her being persistently victimized. At high school a group of '*overbearing*' Year 8 boys made '*gay moves with each other*' and denigrated her in front of her peers. To help gain a sense of belonging, Brooke began acting promiscuously which sadly led to further victimization. At the same time, Brooke was persistently victimized by another female who she believed had '*the power to involve the girls and sort of influence others*'.

> *When they were … when she wasn't in a class with me they* [her peers] *would talk to me and sit next to me and stuff like that … they were 'sorry' … it was like they were torn … like they wouldn't ever want to be treated the way I was but at the same time I think they felt sorry for me.*

Brooke was often physically assaulted by this girl, yet when she disclosed this to her mum, it was suggested that she reside with her aunt who lived 300 kilometres away from Brooke's home town. From Brooke's perspective, such action would have further isolated her, leaving her with no friends and no one to turn to. This was definitely not what she desired, and was not an option.

Unfortunately, Brooke was made to feel responsible for being victimized, therefore she chose to never disclose again and the bullying continued.

> *I remember being in the toilets with her one day and I was just drying my hands and she goes … 'I wouldn't be alone with me … I will bash you …' I'm just like, 'okay' … so I just left.*

Having been severely beaten, the school arranged a meeting with Brooke to discuss how to manage the situation. As a result, Brooke was removed from a number of classes. She explained that '*I don't think they* [the teachers] *knew what to do*' as they also felt intimidated. Despite being removed from certain classes Brooke remained continually taunted by this female who in other settings outside the classroom would sit behind her and cut her hair with scissors. Over time, the bullying moved online, something that is not uncommon (Li 2007; Price et al. 2014; Spears, Slee, Owens & Johnson 2009). Brooke's peers did not intervene, which increased her sense of powerlessness and reinforced her belief that she was to blame. In her eyes, the school's inadequate response sent a clear message to students that bullying was acceptable and this increased the perceived power of the persistent bully. This further reinforced her peers' lack of action as bystanders. Reflecting on these experiences, Brooke proposes actions for schools to employ in addressing persistent bullying.

> *Educating parents ... definitely teachers ... I think they need professional development in the areas ... I think the teachers need to not only be aware but actually care and understand the impact that it can have on their lives ... I think educating people ... all the people that are involved is the most powerful thing that you can do ... and the kids they need almost role play scenarios of things like that to take on different positions and maybe understand how it feels.*

Reasoning that persistent bullies '*need to be able to correct their behaviour*', Brooke encourages schools to adopt '*logical consequences that make sense*' as opposed to excluding persistent bullies from classes or school as she believes the latter will only serve to further boost their reputation and status among peers.

Having experienced persistent victimization, Brooke presents a different perspective to those of other victims, bystanders and bullies. For her, persistent bullying '*comes back to that frustration of just, whether it's jealousy or whether it's just wanting power*'. Brooke proposed that a strong need to belong and '*be recognized ... maybe they want acknowledgement ... those needs of belonging*' motivate and reinforce persistent bullying.

Despite being persistently victimized, Brooke coped and was resilient. Although she described difficult relationships with her parents and some of her peers, there were factors in her life that enabled her to 'bounce back' and cope. Identifying and discussing these factors will provide further insight into Brooke's coping mechanisms.

Risk factors and protective mechanisms

> *I've got to get out of this school just because of the bullying, like uh, suddenly even though I liked my subjects and the peers that I had, the bullying was so bad that I just thought ... how can I keep going?*

A number of factors placed Brooke at risk of being victimized. Firstly, due to her family life, she was perceived as being different in the eyes of the peer group. Various studies have considered family make-up and the relationship between bullying, victims and their families. Some victims, like Brooke, report family relationships that are insecure and often disagreeable (Troy & Sroufe 1987), while others, like Leah (in Chapter 2), describe highly cohesive families (Bowers, Smith & Binney 1994). Studies of victims' families suggest that family members may be more likely to intrude or ignore each other; possibly reflecting poor social and interpersonal skills (Ahmed & Braithwaite 2004). From another perspective, Unnever (2005) found that victims whose parents adopted an authoritarian parenting style, characterized by low acceptance, involvement or autonomy-granting and a high degree of power and control, were less likely to report incidents of bullying, possibly because they viewed the behaviour as normal. Overall it would appear that the relationships that victims share with their families have an impact on how they react to other situations, particularly those involving conflict.

Relationships with peers are also important and can act as a buffer against persistent bullying. The quality and quantity of friendships can potentially determine an individual's risk of being victimized (Rodkin & Hodges 2003), therefore it is important for a child to establish positive dyadic or group relationships. Like Brooke, many victims report feelings of loneliness along with poor social and adjustment skills (Nansel, Overpeck, Pilla, Ruan, Simons-Morton & Scheidt 2001). Victims are less likely to identify with a network of friends and therefore experience a lower perceived social identity than their peers (Cassidy 2009).

Many of Brooke's friends lacked the social skills needed to protect her from further bullying, a common trend among victims (Hodges, Malone & Perry 1997; Pellegrini, Bartini & Brooks 1999; Salmivalli, Huttunen & Lagerspetz 1997). Adding to this, victims – particularly those who are persistently bullied – often lack the confidence and skills to elicit support from peers (Olweus 1978).

Of note, it has been recognized that females are more likely than males to experience negative outcomes associated with long-term bullying (Barker, Arseneault, Brendgen, Fontaine & Maughan 2008; Klomek et al. 2009; Perren, Dooley, Shaw & Cross 2010). These outcomes can include academic failure, negative self-concept, anxiety, depression, low self-esteem, eating disorders and even attempted suicide (Arseneault, Bowes, Shakoor 2010; Baldry & Winkel 2003; Van der Wal, De Wit & Hirasing 2003). Yet, despite being persistently victimized and feeling the need to leave school, Brooke completed Year 12 and entered university to begin her Bachelor of Education. Brooke's ability to cope in the face of adversity was remarkable and leaves one to question how she was able to do this when so many other victims experience negative educational and wellbeing outcomes (Beale 2001). Why do some students like Brooke mature into competent, well-adjusted adults who are successful at school and enter university or achieve other significant goals? Brooke attributes her resilience to sharing close relationships with some of her friends and having a best friend throughout school (Garmezy & Rutter 1983). Adding to this were sporting achievements, such as being elected Sports Captain for three consecutive years and achieving high scores in Year 12.

Today, Brooke describes herself as a tolerant, caring and understanding person who is heavily involved in the church. She is quick to recognize the role played by her faith and her strong connections with other parishioners in helping her to cope during difficult and emotionally stressful times (Garmezy & Rutter 1983; Kim 2008). Religiosity and an affiliation with a church can act as a protective mechanism in the lives of those deemed to be at risk (Kim 2008). For Brooke, this was certainly the case. Within this environment she developed new friendships, gained a sense of belonging and some reprieve from persistent bullying which, in turn, acted as a buffer against her prior negative life experiences (Rutter 1996). Additionally, her high self-esteem and the close relationship that she shared with her younger brother also helped to buffer the negative influences commonly associated with persistent bullying (Bowes, Maughan, Caspi, Moffitt & Arseneault 2010; Sapouna & Wolke 2013). Although studies into the resilience of students who are persistently bullied are scarce (Sapouna & Wolke 2013), Brooke expresses the desire to help young people, similar to herself, foster protective mechanisms that can buffer against persistent bullying.

Chapter summary

Brooke is a seemingly empathetic, tolerant and caring person who has faced many adversities in her life. Relationships are important to her and they have acted as a buffer against these adversities. Acceptance and belonging were important to Brooke, yet despite having a best friend throughout school, she reported feelings of isolation and no sense of belonging. In high school, Brooke acquired the reputation of being 'easy'. While this increased her popularity with the opposite sex, it escalated the victimization she experienced. Thus the need to be accepted – the very thing that was important to Brooke – also appeared to be the catalyst of her persistent victimization. From as young as nine years of age, life experiences led Brooke to be perceived as different, resulting in her victimization. Although Brooke described herself as popular, no one intervened when she was bullied, leaving her feeling isolated and alone. Brooke also described a lack of support from the adults in her life, leading her to believe that she was to blame for the bullying that occurred. Consequently, Brooke did not ask for help and instead apologized for her behaviour, causing the bullying to further escalate. In Brooke's eyes, the school's response, or lack thereof, also appeared to enhance the bully's reputation and reinforce their behaviour. This, she felt, contributed to her ongoing victimization.

As an adult, Brooke has retrospectively provided the voice of someone who was persistently victimized. We can learn from the characteristics and turning points that contributed to Brooke's current status as a competent and well-adjusted young adult. In Chapter 4 we will present the life of Abbie, who self-identifies as a bully/victim.

References

Ahmed, E. & Braithwaite, V. (2004) Bullying and victimization: Cause for concern for both families and schools. *Social Psychology of Education*, 7(1), pp. 35–54.
Arseneault, L., Bowes, L. & Shakoor, S. (2010) Bullying victimization in youths and mental health problems: 'Much ado about nothing'? *Psychological Medicine*, 40(5), pp. 717–729.

Asher, S.R. & Parker, J.G. (1989) The significance of peer relationship problems in childhood. In B. Schneider et al. (eds), *Social competence in developmental perspective*. Dordrecht, The Netherlands: Kluwer Academic Publishers, pp. 5–23.

Baldry, A.C. & Winkel, F.W. (2003) Direct and vicarious victimization at school and at home as risk factors for suicide cognition among Italian adolescents. *Journal of Adolescence*, 26(6), pp. 703–716.

Barker, E.D., Arseneault, L., Brendgen, M., Fontaine, N. & Maughan, B. (2008) Joint development of bullying and victimization in adolescence: Relations to delinquency and self-harm. *Journal of the American Academy of Child & Adolescent Psychiatry*, 47(9), pp. 1030–1038.

Baumeister, R.F. & Leary, M.R. (1995) The need to belong: Desire for interpersonal attachments as a fundamental human motivation. *Psychological Bulletin*, 117(3), pp. 497–529.

Beale, A.V. (2001) Bullybusters: Using drama to empower students to take a stand against bullying behavior. *Professional School Counseling*, 4(4), pp. 300–306.

Bowers, L., Smith, P.K. & Binney, V. (1994) Perceived family relationships of bullies, victims and bully/victims in middle childhood. *Journal of Social and Personal Relationships*, 11(2), pp. 215–232.

Bowes, L., Maughan, B., Caspi, A., Moffitt, T.E. & Arseneault, L. (2010) Families promote emotional and behavioural resilience to bullying: Evidence of an environmental effect. *Journal of Child Psychology and Psychiatry*, 51(7), pp. 809–817.

Bukowski, W.M., Motzoi, C. & Meyer, F. (2009) Friendship as process, function and outcome. In K.W. Rubin, W.M. Bukowski & B. Laursen (eds), *Handbook of peer interactions, relationships and groups*. New York, NY: The Guilford Press, pp. 217–231.

Cassidy, T. (2009) Bullying and victimisation in school children: The role of social identity, problem-solving style, and family and school context. *Social Psychology of Education*, 12(1), pp. 63–76.

Garmezy, N. & Rutter, M. (eds) (1983) *Stress, coping, and development in children*. New York, NY: McGraw Hill.

Hodges, E.V.E., Malone, M.J. & Perry, D.G. (1997) Individual risk and social risk as interacting determinants of victimization in the peer group. *Developmental Psychology*, 33(6), pp. 1032–1039.

Kim, J. (2008) The protective effects of religiosity on maladjustment among maltreated and nonmaltreated children. *Child Abuse & Neglect*, 32(7), pp. 711–720.

Klomek, A.B., Sourander, A., Niemela, S., Kumpulainen, K., Piha, J., Tamminen, T. & Gould, M. (2009) Childhood bullying behaviors as a risk for suicide attempts and completed suicides: a population-based birth cohort study. *Journal of the American Academy of Child and Adolescent Psychiatry*, 48(3), pp. 254–261.

Li, Q. (2007) New bottle but old wine: A research of cyberbullying in schools. *Computers in Human Behavior*, 23(4), pp. 1777–1791.

Nansel, T.R., Overpeck, M., Pilla, R.S., Ruan, W.J., Simons-Morton, B. & Scheidt, P. (2001) Bullying behaviors among US youth: Prevalence and association with psychosocial adjustment. *JAMA: Journal of the American Medical Association*, 285(16), pp. 2094–2100.

Olweus, D. (1978) *Aggression in the schools: Bullies and whipping boys*. Washington, DC: Hemisphere.

Pellegrini, A.D., Bartini, M. & Brooks, F. (1999) School bullies, victims, and aggressive victims: Factors relating to group affiliation and victimization in early adolescence. *Journal of Educational Psychology*, 91(2), pp. 216–224.

Perren, S., Dooley, J., Shaw, T. & Cross, D. (2010) Bullying in school and cyberspace: Associations with depressive symptoms in Swiss and Australian adolescents. *Child and Adolescent Psychiatry and Mental Health*, 4(28). Available from http://dx.doi.org/10.1186/1753-2000-4-28, accessed 20 January 2012.

Price, D., Green, D.M., Spears, B., Scrimgeour, M., Barnes, A., Geer, R. & Johnson, B. (2014) A qualitative exploration of cyber-bystanders and moral engagement. *Australian Journal of Guidance and Counselling*, 24(1), pp. 1–17.

Rodkin, P.C. & Hodges, E.V.E. (2003) Bullies and victims in the peer ecology: Four questions for psychologists and school professionals. *School Psychology Review*, 32(3), pp. 384–400.

Rutter, M. (1996) Transitions and turning points in developmental psychopathology: As applied to the age span between childhood and mid-adulthood. *International Journal of Behavioral Development*, 19(3), pp. 603–626.

Salmivalli, C., Huttunen, A. & Lagerspetz, K.M.J. (1997) Peer networks and bullying in schools. *Scandinavian Journal of Psychology*, 38(4), pp. 305–312.

Sapouna, M. & Wolke, D. (2013) Resilience to bullying victimization: The role of individual, family and peer characteristics. *Child Abuse & Neglect*, 37(11), pp. 997–1006.

Spears, B., Slee, P., Owens, L. & Johnson, B. (2009) Behind the scenes and screens: Insights into the human dimension of covert and cyberbullying. *Journal of Psyhology*, 217(4), pp. 189–196.

Troy, M. & Sroufe, L.A. (1987) Victimization among preschoolers: Role of attachment relationship history. *Journal of the American Academy of Child & Adolescent Psychiatry*, 26(2) pp. 166–172.

Unnever, J.D. (2005) Bullies, aggressive victims, and victims: Are they distinct groups? *Aggressive Behavior*, 31(2), pp. 153–171.

Van der Wal, M.F., De Wit, C.A.M. & Hirasing, R.A. (2003) Psychosocial health among young victims and offenders of direct and indirect bullying. *Pediatrics*, 111(6), pp. 1312–1317.

PART III

The voices of those who bully

4

ABBIE: BULLY/VICTIM

My first day at high school I went to PE and I came back from PE and I went to my schoolbag and my school uniform ... my dress was in there and had all this crap written all over it like for no reason ... I had done nothing at this stage I was just a little Year 8.
(Abbie, 23 years old)

On another occasion 'Abbie' recalls:

I saw her out and I kicked her ... I know that was so wrong of me but I took it out on her ... I said 'how dare you say in front of 40 people my business when you are supposed to be my friend' ... so I kicked her. It was not very nice.

Bully/victims are bullies in some instances and victims in others (Craig 1998; Pellegrini, Bartini & Brooks 1999). Problematically, they make up approximately one-third of the student population and they experience the most severe outcomes of all bullies and victims (Marini, Dane, Bosacki & YLC–CURA 2006). Unlike Abbie, these students are usually physically strong, and more assertive than victims; they are easily provoked and frequently provoke others. They demonstrate high levels of aggression, low academic competence, low prosocial behaviour, low self-control, low social competence and self-esteem, and generally function more poorly than bullies and victims (Batsche & Knoff 1994; Haynie et al. 2001; Veenstra, Lindenberg, Oldehinkel, De Winter, Verhulst & Ormel 2005). Bully/victims view themselves as more troublesome, less intelligent, less physically attractive, more anxious, less popular and unhappier than 'pure' bullies, which impacts on their self-concept (Marini et al. 2006; O'Moore & Kirkham 2001; Schwartz 2000). It is not surprising that these students also report the lowest self-esteem of all groups and hold a very poor self-concept (Olweus 1993; O'Moore & Kirkham 2001). They are most at risk of aggressive behaviours towards their peers (Unnever 2005), are more likely to carry weapons than bullies or victims and are more likely to be victimized by others using weapons (Haynie et al. 2001; Stein, Dukes & Warren 2007).

Chapters 2 and 3 presented the voices of Leah and Brooke who had been victimized at school. The voice of someone who engages in bullying behaviour and is themselves bullied will provide another lens to consider bullying and particularly persistent bullying. Chapter 4 therefore presents the lived experiences and perspectives of Abbie. Prior to our conversation, Abbie had completed an intensive summer school on peer relationships. Part of this course focused on bullying and aggression. With this knowledge and understanding, Abbie identified herself as a bully in some instances and a victim in others which suggests that she was a bully/victim (Salmivalli & Nieminen 2002; Schwartz 2000). She believes that some children get bullied because '*they are easy targets, they don't look like they are very strong … they are not strong characters and people think "oh they're easy targets"*'. For her, the impact of being bullied was devastating. She explains that she couldn't show how she felt as this would lead to further bullying: '*I couldn't even show these people what the effects of going to school was doing to me, I was becoming a shell of a person*'. At home however, Abbie '*would just start crying, I went from someone who was in every sporting activity*' to someone who was depressed and suicidal.

Abbie is 23 years old and in her fourth year of a Bachelor of Education. Abbie's schooling included a co-educational independent primary school, a single-sex independent religious high school, and a Government school in Year 12. She is a relatively petite young lady whose cultural background was different from her peers and this had an effect on her peer relationships as she was often restricted in areas that her peers were not. This left her feeling isolated and lonely. To overcome this, she formed an alliance with others among her peer group who were in a similar situation and together they lied to their parents so that they could socialize and gain a sense of belonging.

Family and peer relationships

Abbie was raised in a family of four: mum, dad and a brother who is eight years older than her. Her parents employed what appeared to be an authoritarian style of parenting: '*you do this and that's the way it is done … you live under my roof*'. In line with this style of parenting, Abbie's parents were strict and expected unquestioning obedience, the preservation of order and tradition and demanded respect for authority (Mussen, Conger, Kagan & Huston 1990; Slee 1993). There was never any discussion about her behavior; Abbie was just told what to do and, when disciplined, '*my dad never said why*' which confused and annoyed Abbie. She saw her parents as strict and felt that she did not have a voice in things that were important to her. While this had a negative impact on her relationships with her parents at the time, she is now reasonably close to them and enjoys spending time with her family.

Like Abbie, many bully/victims report that their families lack cohesion and warmth. Typically, there is a power imbalance between parents, with the father often dominating. Bully/victims tend to be more overprotected or neglected than either bullies or victims (Bowers, Smith & Binney 1994; Smith, Bowers, Binney & Cowie 1993; Stevens, De Bourdeaudhuij & Van Oost 2002). These students perceive their home lives as harsh, disorganized and potentially abusive (Schwartz, Dodge, Pettit & Bates 1997) with unsupportive and uninvolved parents (Schwartz 2000). For Abbie, such family dynamics caused feelings of difference and alienation which possibly influenced her peer interactions.

Bully/victims experience difficulty with peer relationships as they are inclined to attack those who are stronger as well as those who are weaker than them, upsetting the equilibrium of the group. As a result, they are often rejected by the peer group (Schwartz 2000; Warden & Mackinnon 2003). Abbie reported difficulties with her peer relationships which, at times, caused her to feel rejected, victimized and lonely. Although she never had a best friend, Abbie was considered a leader among her peers, much to her own surprise. Being elected as a student representative on the SRC (Student Representative Council) was among her proudest moments. However, mixing with the wrong crowd and engaging in unhealthy behaviours resulted in Abbie losing friends, something that she later regretted. Such behaviour is not uncommon among bully/victims as they search for acceptance and belonging (Kristensen & Smith 2003). When Abbie entered high school she was bullied even more, and she became '*unapproachable*'. She stopped eating and lost interest in everything that once meant a lot to her. Abbie started feeling depressed and suicidal.

> *I lost lots of weight in high school because I just wasn't eating because I was that depressed because I didn't want to go there … and then by the end my grades … 'cause I was pretty good in primary school … Year 8 my grades were okay … by the time I was in Year 11 I was on Ds and I was never … at Year 11 … I was really bad because I think I probably would have committed suicide.*

Ongoing victimization had a significant impact on Abbie's self-esteem and self-concept. At this time, teachers described her as having

> *so many problems they would probably say we didn't notice … there were times I would walk into the classroom crying because someone said they were going to strangle me and my teacher is, like, 'What's wrong?' … I said I just don't want to talk about it but by the end of school they would say 'Yeh she is naughty she is always in trouble' … but at the beginning I was fine.*

Abbie's understandings and experiences of bullying and persistent bullying

Abbie understands bullying to be an ongoing act against another person that includes '*spitting on someone or whatever, but it is verbal … you can really put somebody down*'. Unlike Rebecca and John, whose voices will be heard in later chapters,

Abbie's definition of bullying focuses on repetition and harm, possibly because of the impact that persistent bullying had on her personally. Mirroring her own experiences, Abbie explains that verbal and psychological attacks are more detrimental than physical bullying, something that was also evident in an Australian study of covert bullying by Donna Cross and colleagues (2009).

> *Someone could kick me and I might have been bruised but I would have got on with it, the things that got said to me that 'you're a slut' and you're like this … that really hurts … some things still play in my mind now that people have said.*

Soon after she started school Abbie was victimized by her peers. She was then persistently victimized throughout her school life. As she entered high school the bullying escalated and threats were made against her life.

> *When I would be in the courtyard and they would … you know I am going to slit your throat … At home on the weekends I would get phone calls on my mobile saying 'I'm going to bury you six feet under'.*

Due to her own experiences and the devastating effects of persistent victimization, Abbie believes that bullying should never be seen as a normal part of growing up. In her eyes, differences in popularity and physical appearance invite bullying, aligning with other studies (Frisén, Jonsson & Persson 2007; Sweeting & West 2001; Voss & Mulligan 2000).

> *Some kids get picked on by people who aren't 'in' … all schools have a pecking order … there's the cool people … and then there's the not so cool people the kids that just get picked on by everybody. I don't know, it's sometimes because they're overweight … because they are just easy targets, they don't look like they've got a very strong character and people think oh they're easy targets.*

Most of the bullying that Abbie experienced occurred in the presence of her peers, yet very few intervened, which left her feeling unsupported and powerless. Eventually the bullying escalated, so Abbie avoided areas where the bullies frequented.

Having endured persistent bullying for some time, Abbie turned to her parents for help. Initially her parents blamed her, but as time passed and things didn't change her mum suggested that she ask the girls to stop picking on her. Her father advised that she should '*go straight to the teacher … hang around a teacher if you know that they are coming*'. Unlike Brooke, once Abbie's parents realized the extent of her victimization, they approached the school and actively sought help for her. At this time, Abbie was feeling very depressed and suicidal.

> *I wouldn't want to go … just it depressed me that bad … my behaviour … my attitude, my behaviour towards other people … I was more withdrawn by high school … I stuck to my little group of people and I wouldn't really move out of there.*

As a result of the consultation, Abbie visited the high school counsellor, yet the strategies provided failed and no action was taken against the girls who bullied her. This appeared to send a clear message to the peer group that bullying was acceptable and the bullies were powerful enough to avoid consequences. Concurrently, Abbie started bullying others and by the time she was in Year 9 she bullied others approximately once a week. As mentioned in Chapter 1, Pepler et al. (2008) proposed four bullying trajectories: starts low and increases; starts moderate and desists; starts moderate and remains moderate; and starts high and remains high. Abbie's profile fits the first trajectory of starting low then increasing; she did not engage in bullying when she started school, but by the time she left school she was bullying at moderately high levels.

> I would just be really mean to them ... terrible ... I would do it all the time ... I probably embarrassed them ... it was really not nice to do but I thought, oh well they were lower in the hierarchy ... the pecking order of the school ... there was popular and they were below me so I just took it out on them.

Matching her understandings of why some students are victimized, Abbie targeted students who she perceived as unpopular and lacking power. Through bullying, Abbie increased her power and status among the peer group, which was important to her given that she often felt powerless and desperately needed to be accepted by her peers.

> I thought they're easy targets so I will just take it out on them. They're not going to threaten or strangle me or slit my throat or bury me six feet under ... so I took it out on them.

On one occasion, Abbie physically attacked another student. This incident was reported to the police but no charges were laid. Although Abbie justified her bullying behaviour at the time, she expressed a deep sense of remorse at the time of the interview, something overtly absent in the narrative of both Rebecca, which will be presented in later chapters.

Abbie clearly recognizes the impact of persistent bullying and is in a good place to provide her perspectives and suggestions. She reasons that many factors, particularly one's home life, influence persistent bullying:

> I don't know what their home life is like ... I think they watch too much junk on TV because it's acceptable ... because mum and dad aren't home as much ... but it's not the parents' fault ... we are in financial difficulties ... the parents have to work and kids are in after school care and ... there is the internet as well ... and that is worse ... at least in the old days you bullied at school and then you went home and you slept it off.

To reduce persistent bullying, Abbie recommends developing and fostering a sense of belonging among the school community whereby empathy and tolerance for diversity are embedded. This worked to reduce her own bullying.

> *If there was an overweight child I think they should say look okay obviously John is a little bit overweight but you don't have to be mean ... they could talk to the kids and maybe ... I remember writing a lot of letters about empathy ... really promoting empathy, but what about promoting empathy within your own classroom?*

Based on her own experiences in a single-sex independent religious high school, Abbie queries whether a school's competitive ethos may reinforce persistent bullying. In this setting, she perceived that those who bullied were given specialized treatment due to their academic abilities, in stark contrast to the Government setting where she completed her schooling.

> *What's good for one person is good for everybody but we weren't allowed to have hair colour or nail polish or anything like that ... it was an all girls' Catholic school ... one person would get away with it ... it depends who you were... they [teachers] absolutely had their favourites.*

In addition, there were no consistent consequences for bullying and often bullies were not reprimanded for their behaviour. In Abbie's eyes, this reinforced persistent bullying, sending a message to the peer group that the behaviour was acceptable while adding to the bully's perceived power.

> *No one ever ... no one did anything about it ... the teacher just spoke to me quickly and then 'Oh sorry, I've got too much to deal with'.*

Some teachers were themselves harassed by students which also had an impact on persistent bullying.

> *One poor man ... he was getting picked on by the kids ... he had a really weak personality ... he was really quiet and the kids would give him such a hard time ... they would send him to tears.*

Such intimidation seemingly enhanced the bully's status and power among the peer group and had an impact on Abbie as a victim because she felt unable to talk to anyone or do anything about what was happening. She therefore recommends more professional development for teachers in the area of bullying, particularly conflict management. When considering her own situation, Abbie blamed the school, believing that some teachers escalated bullying situations by what they said or failed to do. She therefore strongly suggests that strict consequences should apply and, more importantly, these consequences should be applied consistently. In fact, studies have found that teachers who view bullies favourably assign blame to the victim (Nesdale & Pickering 2006) which was evident in Abbie's narrative. Popular students have an influence over their peers; bullies who are popular may therefore be less likely to be reprimanded by teachers or their peers for their behaviour (Nesdale & Pickering 2006). A lack of action by teachers informs peers that bullying may be acceptable, which in turn decreases future disclosures (Pepler, personal communication 2012; Unnever & Cornell 2004), a pattern noted in Abbie's case.

Risk factors and protective mechanisms

Why is it that some students who are victimized are at risk of engaging in bullying behaviours? Little is known about the risk and protective factors of this group of students, however it is recognized that bully/victims, like Abbie, tend to display high levels of social anxiety which places them at risk of being both bully and victim (Marini et al. 2006). They are also found to engage in more externalizing or aggressive behaviours as a means of coping with bullying (Kristensen & Smith 2003; Olafsen & Viemerö 2000) which makes them more unpopular with their peers. Consequently, this group of students are also placed at a higher risk of depression, suicidal ideation and poor academic achievement (Haynie et al. 2001), all of which were evident in Abbie's narrative.

So what enabled Abbie to cope and become a successful undergraduate pre-service teacher? There were a number of factors that helped to support her. For instance, she had a group of friends who shared similar cultural backgrounds and together they were able to form an alliance and provide each other with a sense of belonging. She also shared a close relationship with one of her cousins which further provided a sense of belonging and security. This group of friends and her cousin acted as a protective mechanism for Abbie.

Although Abbie's parents did not support her initially, once the effects of bullying escalated in high school they provided her with support which, in turn, helped her to cope. Part of this support resulted in Abbie moving to another school. The new school provided her with a sense of belonging, both with her peers and the school community generally. In this environment Abbie no longer engaged in bullying behaviour nor was she bullied, breaking the cycle and enabling her the space to recover from the effects of previous victimization. Abbie was also proud of her achievements which helped her during the darkest times and reduced the impact of bullying on her self-confidence.

Chapter summary

Abbie's understanding of bullying is underpinned by her own experiences. Although she initially looked to the school for help, no meaningful assistance was provided. She therefore turned to bullying others to gain power and status. During Abbie's high school years her teachers, through favouritism and inconsistent sanctions, appeared to reinforce the power imbalance between bully and victim. Some teachers also felt intimidated and bullied themselves, which appeared to further enhance the power and status of persistent bullies. Abbie highlights the effects of persistent bullying and suggests that family backgrounds may play a large role.

For Abbie, the school ethos played a significant role in either reinforcing or reducing persistent bullying and, by contrasting the two high schools that she attended, she was able to provide insights into strategies that worked and those that did not. These strategies involved a cohesive 'team-like' environment where everyone felt accepted and cared for, together with clear, consistent consequences for bullying. While Abbie bullied others as a result of being victimized herself, some students, like Rebecca and John, bully as a result of peer rejection. Chapter 5 will present the voice and lived experiences of Rebecca who has engaged in bullying behaviour since starting school.

References

Batsche, G.M. & Knoff, H.M. (1994) Bullies and their victims: Understanding a pervasive problem in the schools. *School Psychology Review*, 23(2), pp. 165–175.

Bowers, L., Smith, P.K. & Binney, V. (1994) Perceived family relationships of bullies, victims and bully/victims in middle childhood. *Journal of Social and Personal Relationships*, 11(2), pp. 215–232.

Craig, W.M. (1998) The relationship among bullying, victimization, depression, anxiety, and aggression in elementary school children. *Personality and Individual Differences*, 24(1), pp. 123–130.

Cross, D., Shaw, T., Hearn, L., Epstein, M., Monks, H., Lester, L. & Thomas, L. (2009) *Australian covert bullying prevalence study (ACBPS)*. Perth: Edith Cowan University, Child Promotion Research Centre.

Frisén, A., Jonsson, A.-K. & Persson, C. (2007) Adolescents' perception of bullying: Who is the victim? Who is the bully? What can be done to stop bullying? *Adolescence*, 42(168), pp. 749–761.

Haynie, D.L., Nansel, T., Eitel, P., Crump, A.D., Saylor, K., Yu, K. & Simons-Morton, B. (2001) Bullies, victims, and bully/victims: Distinct groups of at-risk youth. *The Journal of Early Adolescence*, 21(1), pp. 29–49.

Kristensen, S.M. & Smith, P.K. (2003) The use of coping strategies by Danish children classed as bullies, victims, bully/victims, and not involved, in response to different (hypothetical) types of bullying. *Scandinavian Journal of Psychology*, 44(5), pp. 479–488.

Marini, Z.A., Dane, A.V., Bosacki, S.L. & YLC-CURA (2006) Direct and indirect bully-victims: Differential psychosocial risk factors associated with adolescents involved in bullying and victimization. *Aggressive Behavior*, 32(6), pp. 551–569.

Mussen, P.H., Conger, J.J., Kagan, J. & Huston, A.C. (1990) *Child development and personality*. 7th edn. New York, NY: Harper & Row Publishers.

Nesdale, D. & Pickering, K. (2006) Teachers' reactions to children's aggression. *Social Development*, 15(1), pp. 109–127.

Olafsen, R.N. & Viemerö, V. (2000) Bully/victim problems and coping with stress in school among 10- to 12-year-old pupils in Åland, Finland. *Aggressive Behavior*, 26(1), pp. 57–65.

Olweus, D. (1993) *Bullying at school: What we know and what we can do*. Oxford: Blackwell.

O'Moore, A.M. & Kirkham, C. (2001) Self-esteem and its relationship to bullying behaviour. *Aggressive Behavior*, 27(4), pp. 269–283.

Pellegrini, A.D., Bartini, M. & Brooks, F. (1999) School bullies, victims, and aggressive victims: Factors relating to group affiliation and victimization in early adolescence. *Journal of Educational Psychology*, 91(2), pp. 216–224.

Pepler, D.J., Jiang, D., Craig, W.M. & Connolly, J. (2008) Developmental trajectories of bullying and associated factors. *Child Development*, 79(2), pp. 325–338.

Salmivalli, C. & Nieminen, E. (2002) Proactive and reactive aggression among school bullies, victims, and bully-victims. *Aggressive Behavior*, 28(1), pp. 30–44.

Schwartz, D. (2000) Subtypes of victims and aggressors in children's peer groups. *Journal of Abnormal Child Psychology*, 28(2), pp. 181–192.

Schwartz, D., Dodge, K.A., Pettit, G.S. & Bates, J.E. (1997) The early socialization of aggressive victims of bullying. *Child Development*, 68(4), pp. 665–675.

Slee, P.T. (1993) *Child, adolescent and family development*. Marrickville, NSW: Harcourt Brace Jovanovich.

Smith, P.K., Bowers, L., Binney, V. & Cowie, H. (1993) Relationships of children involved in bully/victim problems at school. In S. Duck (ed), *Learning about relationship processes*. London: SAGE, pp. 184–212.

Stein, J.A., Dukes, R.L. & Warren, J.I. (2007) Adolescent male bullies, victims, and bully-victims: A comparison of psychosocial and behavioral characteristics. *Journal of Pediatric Psychology*, 32(3), pp. 273–282.

Stevens, V., De Bourdeaudhuij, I. & Van Oost, P. (2002) Relationship of the family environment to children's involvement in bully/victim problems at school. *Journal of Youth and Adolescence*, 31(6), pp. 419–428.

Sweeting, H. & West, P. (2001) Being different: Correlates of the experience of teasing and bullying at age 11. *Research Papers in Education*, 16(3), pp. 225–246.

Unnever, J.D. (2005) Bullies, aggressive victims, and victims: Are they distinct groups? *Aggressive Behavior*, 31(2), pp. 153–171.

Unnever, J.D. & Cornell, D.G. (2004) Middle school victims of bullying: Who reports being bullied? *Aggressive Behavior*, 30(5), pp. 373–388.

Veenstra, R., Lindenberg, S., Oldehinkel, A.J., De Winter, A.F., Verhulst, F.C. & Ormel, J. (2005) Bullying and victimization in elementary schools: A comparison of bullies, victims, bully/victims, and uninvolved preadolescents. *Developmental Psychology*, 41(4), pp. 672–682.

Voss, L.D. & Mulligan, J. (2000) Bullying in school: Are short pupils at risk? Questionnaire study in a cohort. *British Medical Journal*, 320(7235), pp. 612–613.

Warden, D. & Mackinnon, S. (2003) Prosocial children, bullies and victims: An investigation of their sociometric status, empathy and social problem-solving strategies. *British Journal of Developmental Psychology*, 21(3), pp. 367–385.

5

REBECCA: BULLY

Take whoever is [persistently] bullying to day-care or kindergarten … 'cause there they'll probably learn how to be friends because that's technically where you learn how to be friends … and you're always having fun at kindergarten and day-care.

(Rebecca, eight years old)

Leah, Brooke and Abbie's perspectives highlight that bullying can begin early in life. Chapter 4 concluded the discussions about victimization by presenting the narrative of Abbie, a young adult who identified as being both persistently victimized and engaging in bullying behaviour. Through her voice we gained insight into the many risk factors that contributed to a life of being bullied and bullying others. We also identified a number of protective mechanisms that acted as a buffer against the negative outcomes of persistent bullying. In this chapter we begin to share the perspectives of those who engage in bullying behaviours. Like victims, bullies – particularly persistent bullies – also experience negative outcomes. School-aged bullies have a higher tendency to have a criminal conviction in adulthood (Olweus 1995); are more likely to experience mental health problems such as depression, oppositional conduct disorders and personality defects (Farrington 1993; Kumpulainen, Räsänen & Puura 2001; Olweus 1978; Sourander, Helstelä, Helenius & Piha 2000); are at a greater risk of committing suicide or having suicidal thoughts than victims or others in the peer group (Sampson 2002); tend to underachieve both at school and in later life (Carney & Merrell 2001); and are more likely to engage in alcohol and substance abuse (Farrington 1993; Pepler, Craig, Connolly & Henderson 2001). As adults, they are more likely to adopt anti-social behaviours (Kaltiala-Heino, Rimpelä, Marttunen, Rimpelä & Rantanen 2000; Pulkkinen & Pitkänen 1993) and be aggressive to their spouses (Carney & Merrell 2001). Yet there is currently limited understanding of the factors that reinforce persistent bullying. Therefore, this chapter will begin by presenting the life of 'Rebecca', an eight-year-old girl who identifies as a bully. Her narrative provides insights into the lives of young people who bully.

Rebecca is a Year 3 student who attends a co-educational Government primary school. According to her mum, Rebecca has been diagnosed with an information-processing disorder and experiences *'socialization problems at school which her current teacher has suggested could be labelled as bullying'*.

Family and peer relationships

Rebecca lives with her mum and younger sister, her parents having divorced approximately twelve months prior to our conversation. She misses her dad and visits him each fortnight on court-ordered contact. When reprimanded, she is often found curled up in his chair. Rebecca is closest to her mum, however their relationship is often strained and Rebecca keeps some distance between them. Rebecca's mum employs various disciplinary approaches ranging from negative reinforcement to positive punishment. Rebecca believes that her mum would describe her as '*naughty*', a view that both her mum and her teacher share.

Surprisingly, Rebecca did not choose to start our conversation by talking about her family; instead she discussed her friends. While Rebecca listed five friends, she spoke of them only superficially. Over the course of the conversation she revealed that she often fights with her friends and is frequently left alone. Rebecca's mum highlighted issues with anger management which may explain her difficulties forming and maintaining friendships. Rebecca often described seemingly extreme behaviours.

Friendships have been found to lead to positive social outcomes and behaviours (Howes, Hamilton & Philipsen 1998; Ladd 1990; Sebanc 2003) and the development of social skills such as empathy and sensitivity (Schneider 2000). These skills appear absent in students who engage in bullying behaviours (Arsenio & Lemerise 2001; Endresen & Olweus 2002; Feshbach 1975).

Poor peer relations in early childhood predict social maladaptation in later childhood and adulthood (Asher & Coie 1990; Parker & Asher 1993). While supportive friendships correlate with prosocial behaviours aimed at helping others (Sebanc 2003), negative friendships lead to more negative outcomes. It is therefore crucial for a young child like Rebecca to have positive friendships as these relationships provide an opportunity to learn and practise the necessary skills required to be socially competent. However, this was difficult for Rebecca. Outside of school her only friend is her sister whom she describes as her '*best friend and worst enemy*'. Despite this, she tells how her sister constantly whines because Rebecca has hit, kicked, punched and/or pinched her. These incidents are not isolated to the home as Rebecca is often reprimanded at school for hurting her sister. There have been many times when her sister's friends intervene to protect her.

> *I've got kids in my sister's class that ... kick me and I don't really care. I just try to get away from them ... because my sister calls for help when I just want a hug or a kiss.*

Bullying among siblings is not uncommon. Wolke and Skew (2012) reported that, after reviewing studies of sibling bullying, a startling 50 per cent of participants were involved in bullying their siblings every month and between 16 per cent and 20 per cent engaged in sibling bullying several times a week. Menesini, Camodeca and Nocentini (2010) found that sibling bullying was related to bullying (and victimization) at school. With this in mind, Rebecca's insights and experiences of bullying provide a platform from which we can consider persistent bullying.

Rebecca's understandings and experiences of bullying and persistent bullying

Rebecca was very reluctant to discuss bullying, often speaking in a whisper and not responding without probing questions. She describes bullying as '*being very mean to someone*' through a number of means: '*punch, kick, hit, pinch ... teasing and mimicking*'. In her eyes, bullying differs from a fight because bullying is repetitive and ongoing whereas a fight is not.

> *A fight is when two people do wrestling sometimes. The other kind [bullying] is when you say something ... and then you keep going on and on and on.*

While Rebecca appears to understand that bullying is repetitive and causes harm, her understanding of intentionality is ambiguous. On the one hand, she explains that bullies do not hurt people deliberately – '*they do it because they feel embarrassed*' – however she was unable to elaborate. It is possible that Rebecca is portraying a bully's perspective by minimizing the negative act, thus demonstrating moral disengagement (Bandura 1990). Supporting victims requires students to be morally responsible and adhere to the social conventions of friendship (Price et al. 2014). However, in Rebecca's case, she appears to lack these skills that would otherwise enable her to empathize with victims. In another part of the conversation, Rebecca describes bullying as an intentional act which is motivated by the need to disassociate from someone:

> *'Cause if they focus on one kid then they ... get them out of their life quicker... And if they move on to another kid and then stay on them and then ... they get hurt or injured really bad, they get out of their life quicker again ... the bully leaves them alone because they're not there at school and then the bully would go and find somebody else.*

Although Rebecca's earlier definition of bullying did not acknowledge a power imbalance, in later discussions she explained that in some instances the bully is bigger and/or older than their victim but in others they are not. She clarifies this by saying that '*I've got kids in my sister's class that kick me*'. In general, Rebecca describes all elements of bullying, albeit minimizing intent, possibly to save face (Bandura 1990).

Although Rebecca struggled to remember times or details of incidents of bullying, she recalls being sent to the 'Rethink' room for bullying three times in the past twelve months. One of these times involved an incident with a lifelong friend. This boy was taller than Rebecca but she was older. The two had been friends since birth but the relationship ended abruptly as a result of this incident.

> *We had a fight on the oval … I think it might be my best friend ever … he's seven now, a little bit taller than me and I'm older than him … we met in baby group playgroup when we were only babies … my friend told his teacher. She told me that I had to go up to the Office for a 're-think'.*

Rebecca's mum defines bullying as '*unwanted attention, teasing, aggression or violence towards a person or group on a repeated basis*' and explains '*I think* [Rebecca] *reacts poorly/aggressively to situations* [where] *she feels threatened or out of control*'. Rebecca is aggressive both at home and at school. When provided with a hypothetical scenario of a known bully knocking into her in the tuckshop line, Rebecca did not view the act as intentional. She reasoned: '*in the end they are trying to stop but they have wheels in their shoes and then it's an accident … I'd pick myself up and then pick them up and ask them if that was an accident*'. Such comments align with her view that bullying may not be intentional and instead may be used to cover embarrassment.

Rebecca explains that persistent bullies want to '*show off that they're cool*'. She also considers that some persistent bullies are '*just embarrassed and everyone is looking at them because they think they're big and they look tough but they're not really*'. This reasoning could be interpreted as a way of minimizing her own behaviour.

Rebecca suggests that persistent bullies need to

> *think about all the times that you had that were fun or the times that you have to be told on … and then you think about what's going to happen to you if it hasn't already been happening, then you stop and become friends with them again.*

She also believes that persistent bullies should be taught how to make friends, and schools should '*cast a spell to make everyone be friends*'. If this fails then these students should be expelled. Rebecca has been identified as having relationship difficulties with her peers, therefore it is not surprising that her suggestions centre on developing social skills to enable persistent bullies to gain and maintain friends. Rebecca's views seemingly support Pepler (2006) who argues that bullying is underpinned by relationship issues. Relationship difficulties, along with other internal and external factors, may increase an individual's risk of engaging in bullying behaviour.

Risk factors and protective mechanisms

Many factors can increase an individual's risk of bullying, including temperament and behaviour. Yet it is important to recognize that socio-environmental factors increase this risk over and above individual factors (Bowes, Arseneault, Maughan, Taylor, Caspi & Moffitt 2009). Gaining insight into the lives of those who bully enables risk factors to be identified and explored. While the following discusses potential risk factors that appear to have influenced Rebecca's bullying, they are not necessarily the cause of her aggression. Risk factors interact with the environment and the child's personality and together they potentially increase the likelihood of a child engaging in bullying (Bowes et al. 2009; Orpinas & Horne 2006). Unitary risk factors are unlikely to cause an individual to behave aggressively, however they are more likely to behave this way if multiple risk factors are present (Garmezy 1993). An individual may be predisposed to characteristics that place them at risk of bullying others, such as being impulsive, lacking empathy, needing to dominate others (Olweus 1991), however such characteristics are influenced by relationships with parents and families who may condone aggression, and/or model power-based behaviour (Olweus 1994; Pepler & Sedigheilami 1988). Those who persistently bully have been found to have elevated risks in the individual, parent, peer and relationship domains.

Studies indicate that children who bully are often raised in troubled families by parents who use harsh, unpredictable and often physical discipline (Demaray & Malecki 2003; Dodge, Bates & Pettit 1990; Olweus 1978). Child–parent relationships play a significant role. Rebecca describes a sole parent family where her mother is strict and sets rules and boundaries that cannot be broken. Parents of bullies have consistently been found to adopt this authoritarian style of parenting (Ladd 1992). Such parents are strict, directive and have clear expectations, however they are typically dictatorial and inflexible in their expectations and rules (Slee 1993). Rebecca's relationship with her mother needs to strengthen if Rebecca is to decrease her bullying behaviour; conversely, the further the relationship deteriorates, the more likely her bullying could increase (Orpinas, Murray & Kelder 1999).

Placing Rebecca at further risk are her difficulties socializing with peers. There has been long-standing debate regarding bullies and social skills. Some argue that bullies have specific social skills that enable them to employ peers to support them in one way or another (Arsenio & Lemerise 2001). Others argue that bullies lack social skills (Besag 1989; Olweus 1993). The literature also addresses the way children encode social information, with many arguing that bullying occurs as a result of biases or deficits at one or more of the following stages (Camodeca & Goossens 2005; Crick & Dodge 1994; Dodge 1986):

1. Encoding cues from the situation
2. Interpreting sensory information
3. Clarifying and goal-setting
4. Seeking ideas for possible responses or alternatively developing unique ones

5.   Deciding which response is most appropriate
6.   Following through with the behaviour.

Therefore the way a child reads and responds to a social situation can place them at a higher or lower risk of bullying.

It is not surprising that a lack of friends has also been identified as a risk factor for bullying (see Schneider 2000 for a review). On the one had, children who are overtly aggressive and have high levels of friendship conflict increase their likelihood of future bullying behaviour (Sebanc 2003). In Rebecca's case, her lack of friends appeared to further increase her risk of bullying which in turn increased the rejection that she felt in her peer group. On the other hand, friendships – particularly those low in conflict – can act as a protective buffer against future engagement in bullying.

While bullying is often seen as a negative behaviour, it should also be noted that, for some individuals, bullying can play an adaptive role and achieve desired outcomes, increasing the likelihood of future episodes occurring (Ellis et al. 2012; Perry, Perry & Rasmussen 1986). Individuals are more likely to repeat bullying behaviour if they gain a reward and/or receive little or no punishment. Therefore the perceived outcome of status and belonging can further increase the risk of bullying occurring. Having discussed the potential risk factors, what protective mechanisms can buffer against them?

Protective mechanisms act to reduce or mitigate the impact of risk factors in an individual's life (Rutter 1999). Having strong parent–child relationships, a best friend, close friendships and a sense of belonging to a community can all act as protective mechanisms that will reduce the chance of an individual engaging in bullying behaviour (Orpinas & Horne 2006). While these factors were not evident in Rebecca's life, an improvement in her peer relations could buffer her against further engagement in bullying. It is suggested that if schools help by teaching acceptable or appropriate social skills to all in the peer group, then bullying may be reduced (Pepler 2006). Most anti-bullying interventions focus on reducing risk factors and addressing bullying once it occurs, but it may be more important to help students develop protective mechanisms that can act as buffers. Notably, Rebecca identifies the importance of learning friendship skills in the early years to enhance positive relationship formation and reduce feelings of isolation, thus mitigating against bullying behaviour. We will elaborate on such proactive measures in Chapter 12: *Educational implications.*

Chapter summary

Although relationships are important to Rebecca they are fraught with conflict. She likes to spend time with her family but her relationships with her parents and sister are turbulent. Likewise, Rebecca experiences difficulties with peer relationships. For instance, she lists five friends but was elusive about these relationships. She identified one friend whom she had known since she was a baby but the relationship ended due to what her teachers identified as bullying. In fact, many of her friendships at school ended as a result of conflict. Regrettably, at the time of our conversation, Rebecca did not have a best friend. Outside of school her only friend was her sister whom she described as both her friend and enemy. According to her mum, Rebecca has issues with anger management, possibly explaining her difficulties forming and maintaining friendships. When asked how schools could stop persistent bullying, Rebecca suggested casting a spell to make everyone friends. Rebecca eagerly longed for friendship, however lacked the skills to sustain a mutual relationship.

Despite having a sound understanding of bullying, Rebecca was reluctant to discuss it, often saying '*I don't know*' or '*I can't remember*'. Rebecca cannot decide whether or not bullying is a deliberate act, thus protecting herself and minimizing her own actions. She does not accept responsibility for her own behaviour, a trait that is commonly found in bullies (Menesini, Sanchez, Fonzi, Ortega, Costabile & LoFeudo 2003). She believes that persistent bullying is underpinned by social skill deficits such as poor conflict management skills and difficulties gaining and maintaining friendships, factors which are evident in Rebecca's life. Significantly, Rebecca suggests that persistent bullying is a relationship problem. By sharing her experiences as a bully, Rebecca contributes to our understanding of persistent bullying. Chapter 6 presents the perspective of John who also self-identified as a bully.

References

Arsenio, W.F. & Lemerise, E.A. (2001) Varieties of childhood bullying: Values, emotion processes, and social competence. *Social Development*, 10(1), pp. 59–73.

Asher, S.R. & Coie, J.D. (1990) *Peer rejection in childhood*. Cambridge: Cambridge University Press.

Bandura, A. (1990) Social activation and disengagement of moral control. *Journal of Social Issues*, 46(1), pp. 27–46.

Besag, V.E. (1989) *Bullies and victims in schools: A guide to understanding and management*. Milton Keynes: Open University Press.

Bowes, L., Arseneault, L., Maughan, B., Taylor, A., Caspi, A. & Moffitt, T.E. (2009) School, neighborhood, and family factors are associated with children's bullying involvement: A nationally representative longitudinal study. *Journal of the American Academy of Child & Adolescent Psychiatry*, 48(5), pp. 545–553.

Camodeca, M. & Goossens, F.A. (2005) Aggression, social cognitions, anger and sadness in bullies and victims. *Journal of Child Psychology and Psychiatry*, 46(2), pp. 186–197.

Carney, A.G. & Merrell, K.W. (2001) Bullying in schools: Perspectives on understanding and preventing an international problem. *School Psychology International*, 22(3), pp. 364–382.

Crick, N.R. & Dodge, K.A. (1994) A review and reformulation of social information-processing mechanisms in children's social adjustment. *Psychological Bulletin*, 115(1), pp. 74–101.

Demaray, M.K. & Malecki, C.K. (2003) Perceptions of the frequency and importance of social support by students classified as victims, bullies, and bully/victims in an urban middle school. *School Psychology Review*, 32(3), pp. 471–489.

Dodge, K.A. (1986) A social information processing model of social competence in children. In M. Perlmutter (ed), *The Minnesota Symposia on Child Psychology: Cognitive perspectives on children's social and behavioral development*. Hillsdale, NJ: Erlbaum, pp. 77–125.

Dodge, K.A., Bates, J.E. & Pettit, G.S. (1990) Mechanisms in the cycle of violence. *Science*, 250(4988), pp. 1678–1683.

Ellis, B.J., Del Giudice, M., Dishion, T.J., Figueredo, A.J., Gray, P., Griskevicius, V., Hawley, P.H., Jacobs, W.J., James, J., Volk, A.A. & Wilson, D.S. (2012) The evolutionary basis of risky adolescent behaviour: Implications for science, policy, and practice. *Developmental Psychology*, 48(3), pp. 598–623.

Endresen, I. & Olweus, D. (2002) Self-reported empathy in Norwegian adolescents: Sex differences, age trends, and relationship to bullying. In A.C. Bohart & D.J. Stipek (eds), *Constructive and destructive behavior: Implications for family, school, and society*. Washington, DC: American Psychological Association, pp. 147–165.

Farrington, D.P. (1993) Understanding and preventing bullying. In M. Tonry (ed), *Crime and justice: A review of research, vol. 17*. Chicago, IL: University of Chicago Press, pp. 381–458.

Feshbach, N.D. (1975) Empathy in children: Some theoretical and empirical considerations. *The Counseling Psychologist*, 5(2), pp. 25–30.

Garmezy, N. (1993) Children in poverty: Resilience despite risk. *Psychiatry*, 56(1), pp. 127–136.

Howes, C., Hamilton, C.E. & Philipsen, L.C. (1998) Stability and continuity of child-caregiver and child-peer relationships. *Child Development*, 69(2), pp. 418–426.

Kaltiala-Heino, R., Rimpelä, M., Marttunen, M., Rimpelä, A. & Rantanen, P. (2000) Bullying, depression, and suicidal ideation in Finnish adolescents: School survey. *British Medical Journal*, 319(7206), pp. 348–351.

Kumpulainen, K., Räsänen, E. & Puura, K. (2001) Psychiatric disorders and the use of mental health services among children involved in bullying. *Aggressive Behavior*, 27(2), pp. 102–110.

Ladd, G.W. (1990) Having friends, keeping friends, making friends, and being liked by peers in the classroom: Predictors of children's early school adjustment? *Child Development*, 61(4), pp. 1081–1100.

Ladd, G.W. (1992) Themes and theories: Perspectives on processes in family–peer relationships. In R.D. Park & G.W. Ladd (eds), *Family-peer relationships: Modes of linkage*. Hillsdale, NJ: Erlbaum, pp. 3–34.

Menesini, E., Camodeca, M. & Nocentini, A. (2010) Bullying among siblings: The role of personality and relational variables. *British Journal of Developmental Psychology*, 28(4), pp. 921–939.

Menesini, E., Sanchez, V., Fonzi, A., Ortega, R., Costabile, A. & LoFeudo, G. (2003) Moral emotions and bullying: A cross-national comparison of differences between bullies, victims and outsiders. *Aggressive Behavior*, 29(6), pp. 515–530.

Olweus, D. (1978) *Aggression in the schools: Bullies and whipping boys*. Washington, DC: Hemisphere.

Olweus, D. (1991) Victimization among school children. In R. Baenninger (ed), *Targets of violence and aggression*. Philadelphia, PA: Temple University, pp. 45–102.

Olweus, D. (1993) *Bullying at school: What we know and what we can do*. Oxford: Blackwell.

Olweus, D. (1994) Bullying at school: Basic facts and effects of a school based intervention program. *Journal of Child Psychology and Psychiatry*, 35(7), pp. 1171–1190.

Olweus, D. (1995) Bullying or peer abuse at school: Facts and intervention. *Journal of the American Psychological Society*, 4(6), pp. 196–200.

Orpinas, P. & Horne, A.M. (2006) *Bullying prevention: Creating a positive school climate and developing social competence*. Washington, DC: American Psychological Association.

Orpinas, P., Murray, N. & Kelder, S. (1999) Parental influences on students' aggressive behaviors and weapon carrying. *Health Education & Behavior*, 26(6), pp. 774–787.

Parker, J.G. & Asher, S.R. (1993) Friendship and friendship quality in middle child-hood: Links with peer group acceptance and feelings of loneliness and social dissatisfaction. *Developmental Psychology*, 29(4), pp. 611–621.

Pepler, D.J. (2006) Bullying interventions: A binocular perspective. *Canadian Journal of Child Adolescent Psychiatry*, 15(1), pp. 16–20.

Pepler, D.J. & Sedigheilami, F. (1988) *Aggressive girls in Canada (working paper W98-03E)*. Ottawa: Human Resources Development Canada.

Pepler, D.J., Craig, W., Connolly, J. & Henderson, K. (2001) Bullying, sexual harassment, dating violence, and substance use among adolescents. In C. Wekerle & A. Wall (eds), *The violence and addiction equation: Theoretical and clinical issues in substance abuse and relationship violence*. Philadelphia, PA: Brunner/Mazel, pp. 153–168.

Perry, D.G., Perry, L.C. & Rasmussen, P. (1986) Cognitive social learning mediators of aggression. *Child Development*, 57(3), pp. 700–711.

Price, D., Green, D.M., Spears, B., Scrimgeour, M., Barnes, A., Geer, R. & Johnson, B. (2014) A qualitative exploration of cyber-bystanders and moral engagement. *Australian Journal of Guidance and Counselling*, 24(1), pp. 1–17.

Pulkkinen, L. & Pitkänen, T. (1993) Continuities in aggressive behavior from childhood to adulthood. *Aggressive Behavior*, 19(4), pp. 249–263.

Rutter, M. (1999) Resilience concepts and findings: Implications for family therapy. *Journal of Family Therapy*, 21(2), pp. 119–144.

Sampson, R. (2002) Bullying in schools. Problem-oriented guides for police series (no. 12). Available from www.cops.usdoj.gov, accessed 3 January 2012.

Schneider, B.H. (2000) *Friends and enemies: Peer relations in school*. London: Arnold.

Sebanc, A.M. (2003) The friendship features of preschool children: Links with prosocial behavior and aggression. *Social Development*, 12(2), pp. 249–268.

Slee, P.T. (1993) *Child, adolescent and family development*. Marrickville, NSW: Harcourt Brace Jovanovich.

Sourander, A., Helstelä, L., Helenius, H. & Piha, J. (2000) Persistence of bullying from childhood to adolescence – a longitudinal 8-year follow-up study. *Child Abuse & Neglect*, 24(7), pp. 873–881.

Wolke, D. & Skew, A.J. (2012) Bullying among siblings. *International Journal of Adolescent Medicine and Health*, 24(1), pp. 17–25.

6

JOHN: PERSISTENT BULLY

My whole schooling life was just trouble … one point the deputy head master expected me in his office so often that he would have a pile of work for me to do and he wouldn't even ask me what I did wrong … he would just say 'Oh [John] take this and …'

(John, 26 years old)

Persistent bullying can unfortunately become a natural and expected behaviour – not only from the bully's perspective, but also from those surrounding and responsible for them. One may question how this can actually come to be? Chapter 5 shed light on the life of a young girl who engaged in bullying behaviour. Her voice provided insight into potential risk and protective factors that influenced and shaped her life and behaviour. This chapter builds on this understanding by presenting the voice of a young man who persistently bullied others throughout his school life. We aim to deepen current knowledge of persistent bullying in order to inform efforts to proactively address such behaviour.

'John' is 26 years old and enrolled in a postgraduate teaching degree at university. During his schooling, he attended a number of co-educational independent schools; the primary schools were relatively small but the high schools were large. John's mother taught at the schools that John attended. Although she was never his teacher, he describes being '*sent to her room when I was misbehaving*'. Each time his mother changed schools John would also move, which resulted in numerous transitions, something he found very difficult. From a young age John did not enjoy school. He struggled with relationships both in and out of school which left him lacking a sense of belonging. As he matured he also struggled to find his identity.

Family and peer relationships

John described his family memories reasonably positively, albeit rather superficially. As an adult, he enjoys a relatively close relationship with his mum and younger brother, yet this is not the case with his father or sisters. During his childhood John's parents, like Abbie's, employed an authoritarian parenting style where strict rules were enforced and misdemeanours managed without consultation or discussion (Maccoby & Martin 1983). In line with this parenting style, John's parents expected unquestioning obedience. John vividly recalled:

> *one thing, we would have to play the piano every day, um, and as kids we didn't want to play the piano ... Yeah, it was half an hour every day so anytime that we weren't playing was being timed, so we would have to do it and we couldn't watch TV or we wouldn't do something fun; it was basically we had to do it or ...*

Consequences for misbehaviour often involved positive punishment such as a smack. John felt that his parent's power and authority were usually enough to ensure that he did what he was told.

> *It was definitely ... I had to follow the rules ... it was basically we had to do it.*

Sadly, John's parents did not hold a high opinion of him and when he got into trouble at school his parents were never shocked – in fact, they often expected it. Not surprisingly, during his school years John did not share a particularly close relationship with either parent, therefore in seeking a sense of belonging he turned to his peers.

Regrettably, even though John sought friendships with his peers, right from an early age he experienced their rejection, which continued throughout his school life:

> *It was sort of a game ... to run away from me and every lunchtime ... I remember one time I got so upset I ran out of the school grounds crying and they came and found me and told the teacher '[John's] out of bounds, you know you've got to tell him off'.*

In an attempt to help John make friends, his teacher would pair him with any new students who arrived at the school. However, after a day or so, the peer group would encourage the new student to exclude John and he was again rejected. This further exacerbated his lack of belonging within the peer group and increased his sense of loneliness.

> *When a new kid came the teacher said 'Oh [John], can you come and show this student around' ... I think it was trying to make friends ... and for the first day or so he was, but then at lunchtime the students were saying 'No, no, you have to run away from him' and so he sort of 'Oh okay' and joined in so that was the end of that.*

During this time there was a small group of boys who would constantly make fun of John, something he found distressing. School, particularly primary school, was very difficult for him:

> *That, combined with some of the bad teachers as well … some years were terrible. I remember saying 'I don't want to go'.*

Being bigger than his peers, John began to allow others to physically wrestle him so that it would provide him with some sense of connection and belonging, as opposed to being excluded.

> *I was much bigger than those other boys … we would do some sort of wrestling so everyone versus [John] sort of thing, physically.*

Despite his strong need to belong, John continued to be rejected and frequently changed friendship groups in an attempt to be accepted. Throughout school, John had only one friend which was a very short-lived relationship. Both boys bullied others and derived enjoyment from this. For John, being accepted and popular among his peers was important. Engaging in disruptive and bullying behaviours, he believed, enhanced his identity and status among the peer group. John was often punished for these behaviours which he felt further enhanced his image of being 'cool'.

John's understandings and experiences of bullying and persistent bullying

Due to the constant rejection from his peers, John started bullying others and in high school he joined others who bullied. Throughout his school life he consistently engaged in moderate to high levels of bullying.

> *I was the student that would get into trouble and that involved … making other students feel bad … I remember in Reception I would steal people's lunches from them while they were eating … I would fit in that category* [moderate to high levels of bullying] *from the beginning.*

John understands bullying to be:

> *Where a student or a few students make another student feel bad or do bad things to the other student for some sort of satisfaction or some sort of gain.*

John astutely recognized elements of intent and power in his definition of bullying; however, he focused on the bully's outcomes or justifications, as opposed to the impact on the victim. John minimized the impact of bullying by explaining that some students are successful in life as a result of being bullied.

> *I think some of the kids who are bullied are very successful ... because of that ... and some kids who never had confrontations in school don't know how to deal with it outside of school ... I think it develops a certain type of skill in students or tolerance ... I think in some ways for a person to get to where they are they have had to have gone through or go through what they have gone through ... for some students that's bullying ... I think it teaches them certain life abilities or life skills so they can deal with certain things a lot more.*

John describes a victim as:

> *someone who doesn't have the skills to retaliate ... whether they can't think of the right things to say or they're too shy or their reaction is too strong ... they don't know how to control their reaction ... they don't have the people skills to get any support from any of the class members in their response to bullying ... They [their peers] see them as a bit of a loser, maybe weak as well ... definitely on the loser side of things.*

John diffuses the impact of his own behaviour and vilifies the victim by believing that they deserve to be bullied (Bandura 1999; Bandura, Barbaranelli, Caprara & Pastorelli 1996; Hymel, Rocke-Henderson & Bonanno 2005). He also portrays victims as inept in terms of strength and social skills. Such perceptions may have been accrued due to his own experiences.

When asked to describe bullies, John identifies two types:

> *Someone who's a bit of a ringleader in a class who'll spearhead an attack on someone ... sort of have the class generally behind them ... another bully is someone who has not much respect at all by the class but still goes around and does that type of thing anyway ... maybe has one or two friends but generally is the outsider ... so it could be a popular bully or it could be an outsider, an unpopular bully.*

John self-identifies as a persistent bully who lacks respect *for* others and is not respected *by* others.

Although John primarily describes himself as a persistent bully, he also mentions times when he was victimized at school. In Year 5/6 John was victimized by his same-age peers as well as older students. The majority of this bullying was verbal; however, there were times when it was physical. Understandably, this was a very unhappy period for John. At the time he believed that retaliation would '*change something in their mind ... which would stop it*'. Paradoxically, at the same time John was bullying those weaker than himself, suggesting he may have been a bully/victim.

When John started school, he was bullying at a low level, however this soon escalated. In Reception, at the age of five, he stole other students' lunches and engaged in other bullying activities. At this time, the school approached his parents and, with their permission, he was caned as punishment. Perhaps such physical punishment influenced John's subsequent behaviours? For example, in Years 4 and 5 John recalls belonging to a group of students who were not friends but who grouped together to physically attack others.

> There was an incident where this kid was getting pushed around and a bottle got thrown at his head but that was actually from our small group of bullies and the kid ended up going off in the toilets.

At the end of Year 8 and the beginning of Year 9, John befriended a boy who had migrated from South Africa. Both boys were large in stature and held considerable power over their peers. Together they taunted and bullied others, particularly those who were considered different.

> One was a bit nerdy ... he was very good at studying ... he was that type of kid who would study hard ... he was very smart ... another kid who we picked on didn't have good people skills; he ... couldn't interact properly with other students ... even when we weren't causing him trouble ... he would cause himself trouble in class ... some of the other kids just associated with those kids ... one guy in particular had a physical feature that wasn't so normal.

John justified his behaviour by reasoning that these students were bullied by others and that they deserved to be bullied. John explained that he engaged in two types of bullying:

> There was different types of bullying ... the light-hearted bullying which did affect the kids ... we didn't think so at the time ... then the other bullying where we would do it for our fun not for the class's fun and that was a bit more negative I think.

Both types were underpinned by 'fun' and personal enjoyment.

> It would be a comment that seemed clever ... it didn't seem so negative ... it was just a bit light-hearted that got the whole class to laugh ... but it seemed like we set out to make those other kids feel bad.

John remained rejected by his peers and believed that bullying would enhance his identity and sense of belonging. In line with this, John felt that bullying would not occur without an audience.

John was oblivious to the pain and distress he was causing and, on one occasion, a teacher explicitly explained the impact of his behaviour on a particular student. The aim was to encourage John to understand the victim's perspective and feel some empathy towards him:

> There was another situation where I'd bullied a kid just verbally in class and the teacher pulled me aside and said, 'You know that kid normally comes and talks to me every day after school but he went home without talking to me because he was so upset' ...

and he really talked me through it from that perspective and showed how he was disappointed in me … that changed it for me actually … I stopped bullying that kid … I was a bit sorry for what I had done.

This had a greater impact than any punishment and John stopped bullying that particular student. However, John continued to bully others for the remainder of his school life. Through the teacher's explicit description of the student's pain, John was able to empathize with the victim, yet he seemed unable to generalize to other situations. The teacher's strategy therefore had no impact on his behaviour towards other students.

John could not recollect any specific anti-bullying interventions employed by the schools he attended. In primary school, students had lessons on bullying which, in his eyes, were ineffective. He proposed that these strategies served to further enhance his standing as a bully within the peer group. However, he did emphasize the role that respect and good student–teacher relationships can play in deterring persistent bullying. For him, the key to reducing persistent bullying involves helping students develop empathy for others, something he struggled with. He suggested that units of work on bullying should be '*really personal to the incidents that happen*' as opposed to merely learning that bullying '*makes the kids feel bad*'.

In high school John received several detentions because of persistent bullying but he was never suspended. These punishments enhanced his identity, power and status among his peers. Further, they helped to fulfil his needs and consequently did not deter his behaviour. Therefore John does not think that punishment is the answer as persistent bullies come to expect it and this informs their self-view. John's comments suggest that caution is needed if school staff are tempted to apply labels such as 'bully' and 'victim'. Such classifications may constrain children as well as influence the way others think about and treat them, possibly reinforcing their behaviour. John further counsels that discussions between the teacher, bully and victim should be conducted in private to avoid further enhancing the bully's status among peers.

What factors reinforce persistent bullying?

So what placed John at risk of engaging in persistent bullying? Research suggests that rejection, and lacking a sense of belonging and connectedness not only places a person at risk of bullying others but also motivates and reinforces anti-social behaviours such as persistent bullying (Baumeister & Leary 1995; Österman 2000) as evident in John's life. For him, bullying was a means of entertaining his peers, thus gaining their attention and providing him with an identity.

It was not surprising that John could not think of anything he liked at school, however outside school he enjoyed a range of sports and played the drums which seemingly enhanced his identity.

I really liked the drums as well and the image that went along with it … to be seen as the drummer was cool … that was cool.

The importance of establishing an identity and reputation of being 'cool' was emphasized throughout John's narrative. Therefore, when we look at persistent bullying, we need to consider the role that significant others play. Could their behaviours, perceptions and beliefs actually reinforce bullying for some individuals? Inadvertently, teachers – and particularly the punishments they delivered – seemingly enhanced John's reputation and image among his peers, thus reinforcing his bullying behaviour. For John, the punishments he received at school helped him fulfil his social goals.

> *I think punishments sometimes are a bit of an identity ... as well I remember going to detention all the time and seeing the same kids and we would talk in class ... it was sort of a group you know 'the detention kids' ... 'Oh what did you do?' ... we didn't really care and if you got punished it was just because I'm bad ... that's who I am ... you can brush it off pretty easily I think, and it helps to create who you are as well.*

Being one of the '*detention kids*' appeared to fulfil John's need to belong and enhanced his status and reputation among his peer group. John had many behavioural problems at school, most of which were motivated by his need for peer group status and acceptance. The need to belong and be accepted by his peers appeared to outweigh his empathy for those he victimized.

John was regularly held responsible for aberrant behaviours, even when he was not involved. He was identified by peers, teachers and other school staff as 'trouble' and a 'bully', and even his mother shared this view. While parents can often buffer against the negative views of others by seeing their children in a positive light, John's parents actually confirmed these negative perceptions, adding detrimentally to his self-concept. These negative descriptors became so entrenched in his self-view that, even as a university student, he still used the terms 'trouble' and 'bully' to describe himself.

John held teachers and the schools he attended responsible for his persistent bullying, explaining that students may bully because they are bored or rejected by their peers. Further to this, John explained that the attributions made by the school principal(s), teachers, peers and their parents and even his own parents played a large role in shaping his behaviour and the way that he saw himself:

> *I think a lot of it comes down to identity ... who the student thinks they are ... is a big part of it ... which is brought about by the teachers and the school.*

John contends that students persistently bully because they need to enhance their identity and sense of belonging within the peer group. In his case, the attitude and behaviour of stakeholders in the school enhanced John's self-image.

John also explained that many factors underpin persistent bullying:

> *Who the student thinks they are is a big part of it which is brought about by the teachers and the school ... but I guess it's also in the bully as well to do it ... but maybe it's*

> *that lack of fear for authority that is a part of it … they don't care about the school's authority.*

Consistent with reports of bullying across the world, John expresses an intense desire to be seen as 'cool', 'tough' and powerful (Mishna 2004; Sutton, Smith & Sweetham 1999). Being recognized by teachers and other stakeholders as a bully provides an identity, albeit negative, which can be self-fulfilling (Rosenthal & Jacobson 1968). Concurrently, the label of bully becomes part of the student's self-concept which establishes a negative self-view. Subconsciously, through their actions, the student works to verify and reinforce this negative identity (North & Swann 2009) (refer to Figure 6.1). Thus, as John consistently emphasized, others can positively or negatively influence an individual's self-concept and behaviour. For him, these perceptions fulfil his social goals of status and identity. If bullying meets the needs of persistent bullies, there is no motive for them to change their behaviour (Ellis et al. 2012; Hawley 2011).

Within an educational context the problem of persistent bullying is complex. Teachers can inadvertently reinforce the behaviour by their actions and interactions with bullies and victims (Hughes & Cavell 1999; Hughes, Cavell & Willson 2001;

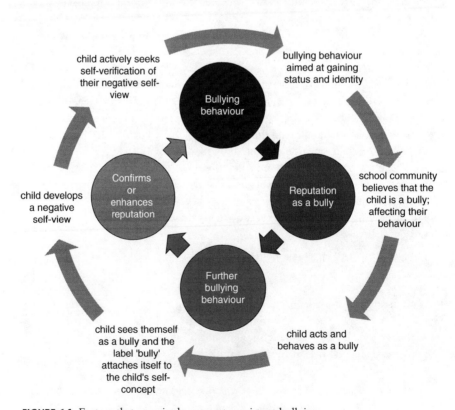

FIGURE 6.1 Factors that seemingly support persistent bullying

Madon et al. 2001). Teachers and counsellors report that dealing with student bullying causes them increased stress and fatigue (Green 2015). If students are attuned to this, the peer group power and status of bullies could be increased, potentially fulfilling their goals and reinforcing persistent bullying. Yet ignoring bullying may send a message that the behaviour is considered acceptable.

Empathy seemingly forms part of the puzzle of why some students persistently bully. Recognizing the negative impact that bullying has on others can be enough to stop some bullies (Jolliffe & Farrington 2006). John described situations where he was unaware of others' pain. Even after a teacher explicitly explained the impact of his behaviour, John was either unable or unwilling to stop bullying. John's lack of empathy simultaneously contributed to his peer rejection and exacerbated it (Saliquist, Eisenberg, Spinrad, Eggum & Gaertner 2009), setting up a cycle. Retrospectively, he appeared to regret his actions, yet he was unable to recognize his victims' pain at the time.

Evidently several factors work together to motivate and reinforce persistent bullying. Lacking empathy and needing acceptance may initiate bullying but others' perceptions seemingly reinforce the behaviour. Persistent bullying is further reinforced when the behaviour fulfils the individual's social goals (Ellis et al. 2012; Hawley 2011).

Chapter summary

John demonstrated a sound understanding of bullying yet, like many bullies, appeared to vilify his victims as a means of justifying his behaviour. Pepler and her colleagues (2008) identified similar individual characteristics in students who were high on the bullying trajectory. These students were more inclined to be morally disengaged and experience serious problems in their peer relationships. Rejection throughout school led John to bully his peers as a way of gaining status and a sense of belonging. Punishment enhanced his status and served to meet his need to be seen as powerful.

Bullying behaviour has several negative developmental outcomes, including: rejection (Coie, Dodge & Kupersmidt 1990); academic difficulties (Carney & Merrell 2001); higher levels of criminal involvement; and engagement in risky behaviour (Farrington 1993; Pepler, Craig, Connolly & Henderson 2001). However, risky behaviours such as bullying can be adaptive and have positive outcomes for an individual (Ellis et al. 2012; Hawley 2011). In John's case, bullying provided a sense of belonging, status, power and identity, which he was unable or unwilling to achieve in other ways. From John's perspective, bullying provided positive outcomes including enjoyment and prestige. When taking this view, it is understandable that some bullies may be reluctant to change their behaviour.

When discussing persistent bullying, John suggested the need to develop empathy. He described a time when the impact of his behaviour was explicitly explained by a teacher, and while this enabled him to empathize with that student, he was not able to transfer this emotion to other victims. Is it possible that persistent bullies have not seen or learnt the necessary social skills that underpin empathy, resulting in an inability to naturally experience empathy and/or transfer these feelings? If so, interventions that aim to teach empathy may need further consideration.

In John's eyes, many people played a role in reinforcing his persistent bullying. In particular, he identified the attributions made by others coupled with the way he saw himself as playing a major role. Others' attributions helped to shape his reputation among peers, therefore he continued to act in a way that reinforced this identity and peer reputation. He believes that other people's attitude and behaviour towards him served to confirm his image of a '*trouble kid*' and a bully. Their attitudes and actions also sent a clear message to the peer group who then saw John in this light. Over time, John began to think of himself as a bully, which unfortunately contributed to his persistent bullying.

Part III has presented the voices of a bully/victim, a bully and a persistent bully. However, childhood bullying rarely occurs without an audience, thus Chapters 7, 8 and 9 provide a segue into the lives, experiences and understanding of bystanders.

References

Bandura, A. (1999) Moral disengagement in the perpetration of inhumanities. *Personality and Social Psychology Review*, 3(3), pp. 193–209.

Bandura, A., Barbaranelli, C., Caprara, G.V. & Pastorelli, C. (1996) Mechanisms of moral disengagement in the exercise of moral agency. *Journal of Personality and Social Psychology*, 71(2), pp. 364–374.

Baumeister, R.F. & Leary, M.R. (1995) The need to belong: Desire for interpersonal attachments as a fundamental human motivation. *Psychological Bulletin*, 117(3), pp. 497–529.

Carney, A.G. & Merrell, K.W. (2001) Bullying in schools: Perspectives on understanding and preventing an international problem. *School Psychology International*, 22(3), pp. 364–382.

Coie, J.D., Dodge, K.A. & Kupersmidt, J.B. (1990) Peer group behaviour and social status. In S.R. Asher & J.D. Coie (eds), *Peer rejection in childhood*. New York, NY: Cambridge University Press, pp. 17–59.

Ellis, B.J., Del Giudice, M., Dishion, T.J., Figueredo, A.J., Gray, P., Griskevicius, V., Hawley, P.H., Jacobs, W.J., James, J., Volk, A.A. & Wilson, D.S. (2012) The evolutionary basis of risky adolescent behaviour: Implications for science, policy, and practice. *Developmental Psychology*, 48(3), pp. 598–623.

Farrington, D.P. (1993) Understanding and preventing bullying. In M. Tonry (ed), *Crime and justice: A review of research, vol. 17*. Chicago, IL: University of Chicago Press, pp. 381–458.

Green, D.M. (2015) An investigation of persistent bullying at school: Multiple perspectives of a complex social phenomenon. Doctoral dissertation, University of South Australia.

Hawley, P.H. (2011) The evolution of adolescence and the adolescence of evolution: The coming of age of humans and the theory about the forces that made them. *Journal of Research on Adolescence*, 21(1), pp. 307–316.

Hughes, J.N. & Cavell, T.A. (1999) Influence of the teacher-student relationship in childhood conduct problems: A prospective study. *Journal of Clinical Child Psychology*, 28(2), pp. 173–184.

Hughes, J.N., Cavell, T.A. & Willson, V. (2001) Further support for the developmental significance of the quality of the teacher–student relationship. *Journal of School Psychology*, 39(4), pp. 289–301.

Hymel, S., Rocke-Henderson, N. & Bonanno, R.A. (2005) Moral disengagement: A framework for understanding bullying among adolescents. *Journal of Social Sciences*, 8(1), pp. 1–11.

Jolliffe, D. & Farrington, D.P. (2006) Examining the relationship between low empathy and bullying. *Aggressive Behavior*, 32(6), pp. 540–550.

Maccoby, E.E. & Martin, J.A. (1983) Socialization in the context of the family: Parent–child interaction. In P.H. Mussen & E.M. Hetherington (eds), *Handbook of child psychology (vol. 4): Socialization, personality and social development*. 4th edn. New York, NY: Wiley, pp. 1–101.

Madon, S., Smith, A., Jussim, L., Russell, D.W., Eccles, J., Palumbo, P. & Walkiewicz, M. (2001) Am I as you see me or do you see me as I am? Self-fulfilling prophecies and self-verification. *Personality and Social Psychology Bulletin*, 27(9), pp. 1214–1224.

Mishna, F. (2004) A qualitative study of bullying from multiple perspective. *Children & Schools*, 26(4), pp. 234–247.

North, R.J. & Swann, W.B. (2009) Self-verification 360°: Illuminating the light and dark sides. *Self and Identity*, 8(2–3), pp. 131–146.

Österman, K.F. (2000) Students' need for belonging in the school community. *Review of Educational Research*, 70(3), pp. 323–367.

Pepler, D., Craig, W., Connolly, J. & Henderson, K. (2001) Bullying, sexual harassment, dating violence, and substance use among adolescents. In C. Wekerle & A. Wall (eds), *The violence and addiction equation: Theoretical and clinical issues in substance abuse and relationship violence*. Philadelphia, PA: Brunner/Mazel, pp. 153–168.

Pepler, D.J., Jiang, D., Craig, W.M. & Connolly, J. (2008) Developmental trajectories of bullying and associated factors. *Child Development*, 79(2), pp. 325–338.

Rosenthal, R. & Jacobson, L. (1968) Pygmalion in the classroom. *The Urban Review*, 3(1), pp. 16–20.

Saliquist, J., Eisenberg, N., Spinrad, T., Eggum, N.D. & Gaertner, B.M. (2009) Assessment of preschoolers' positive empathy: Concurrent and longitudinal relations with positive emotion, social competence, and sympathy. *The Journal of Positive Psychology*, 4(3), pp. 223–233.

Sutton, J., Smith, P.K. & Sweetham, J. (1999) Bullying and 'theory of mind': A critique of the 'social skills deficit' view of anti-social behaviour. *Social Development*, 8(1), pp. 117–127.

PART IV

The voices of those who are uninvolved

7

SAMANTHA: DESISTER

I met one of my best friends when we were four in Kindy ... and it was sort of me and her against the world ... somehow we were just drawn to each other ... and we were friends from then on and ... I think because we were bullied by our brothers and sisters we started bullying ... I remember even in Kindy my friend said 'Oh let's put water in this girl's bag' so we got some water and tipped it in this girl's bag.

(Samantha, 27 years old)

In Part IV, *Multiple Perspectives in Persistent Bullying: Capturing and listening to young people's voices* shifts to present the insights of those who had been involved in bullying behaviours, however were uninvolved at the time of our conversations. Chapter 7 will commence by discussing the life of 'Samantha' who started bullying at low levels in kindergarten but desisted as she entered Year 4. We contrast her lived experiences with those of Abbie, a bully/victim (Chapter 4), Rebecca, a bully (Chapter 5) and particularly John, a persistent bully (Chapter 6) in order to gain insight into the potential differences between those who desist and those who persist.

The 'desister', who commences bullying behaviour but stops over time, is one of the four bullying trajectories outlined by Pepler and her colleagues (2008). Like those who have never engaged in bullying, desisters typically experience fewer problems with moral disengagement and aggression, and demonstrate low conflict with parents and peers (Pepler et al. 2008). Using Pepler et al.'s (2008) trajectories, Samantha identified herself as a desister, saying '*I think I bullied until about Year 4 and then I stopped*'.

Samantha is a 27-year-old undergraduate in her fourth year of a Bachelor of Education degree. She attended a large Government primary and high school until Year 11 when she moved to a co-educational Catholic school. She liked the cohesive climate that existed in the Catholic school as '*there was a real sense of community'*. Later, Samantha identified community as a factor in reducing persistent bullying, a view that was also shared by Abbie.

Samantha was quick to articulate her academic achievements as among her proudest moments. However, she regretted growing up too fast and getting *'into the drinking and taking drugs when I was pretty young'*. Samantha describes a happy home life and shared close relationships with her immediate and extended family to whom she could turn for help or advice.

Family and peer relationships

Samantha is the youngest member of her extended family and, as a child, was spoilt by adults and teased and *'picked on by the kids'*. She attributes her early bullying behaviour to this teasing. She feels closest to her mum, both during her school life and into adulthood. Her mother was very involved in her life: *'Mum would always take me on trips and stuff'* which possibly contributed to their close relationship. Samantha also shares a close relationship with her older brother. However, despite getting on well with her dad, they were not close – possibly because they were too much alike. Samantha feels that she could turn to any member of her immediate or extended family for help and they would be there for her.

When talking about parenting styles, Samantha identified her parents as being either laissez-faire or authoritative. Laissez-faire parents tend to offer little guidance about behaviour, rarely set limits, and believe that there is little that can be done about negative behaviour. Authoritative parents are warm but firm, set clear standards and have high expectations of their children. These parents use a rational and democratic approach which involves verbal give-and-take between child and parent.

> *Yeh so they were pretty laid back and sort of let us, both me and my brother … do things and then, oh it was like, I don't know how they knew we'd end up doing it, but eventually we'd work out 'Okay this is wrong' for ourselves.*

In line with this approach, Samantha's parents employed a relaxed method of discipline where the 'rules' were never explained: *'they never sat down and said these are the rules of the house but we sort of just knew, I guess, by their behaviour'*. Yet due to the respect she had for her parents she often hears their words of warning, even today as an adult.

If Samantha got into trouble at school, her parents talked to her about what she had done. They encouraged her to be empathetic by saying *'How would you feel if someone did this to you … This is how you are making these people feel'*. This approach helped Samantha develop empathy for others, which in turn seemingly had a positive impact on her peer relationships.

Samantha had lots of close friendships throughout her school life and some of these were retained into adulthood. At the age of four, Samantha had a best friend and they did everything together. She had the feeling that it was *'me and her against the world'*.

I have always had two really close friends since I was born and then one from when I was four, so even though they didn't go to the same high school we're still friends today and they were friends throughout high school as well.

Samantha was reasonably popular throughout school; however she never followed the pack and often stood up for what she believed, even if this meant losing friends, thus identifying as somewhat 'controversial' (Coie & Dodge 1988).

I've always been popular but if I don't like something I'll let it be known I won't just go along with things ... I just won't put up with stuff whereas, I think yeah a lot of people just go along with things ... they have a lot of friends because they do whatever the head person says.

Feeling confident in herself, she chose to attend a different high school to her friends which supported the extension of her friendship circle. She transitioned to another school again in Year 11, however – unlike John – this did not seem to worry her as she quickly established new friends and felt a strong sense of belonging. Samantha's understandings of bullying provide a different lens to Rebecca, John and Abbie as she had engaged in bullying behaviour and then desisted.

Samantha's understandings and experiences of bullying and persistent bullying

Like Abbie, at the time of our conversation Samantha had just completed a summer school that focused on peer relationships. Bullying and victimization were explicitly addressed in this course, therefore it was not surprising that her understandings of bullying aligned closely to the literature in this area:

It's a behaviour that could be one person does to another person or five people do to another person. For that person it's inappropriate and that person doesn't like it. It could be teasing them or hitting them or just ignoring them or something that affects that person negatively ... I don't even know if it has to be ongoing; I think sometimes just single incidents can be bullying as well.

Samantha expresses a clear understanding of both intent and power imbalance, yet questions repetition, something that has also been debated in the literature (e.g. Guerin & Hennessey 2002). Like Samantha, some scholars suggest that perceived intent is enough to qualify as bullying. Samantha differentiates bullying from a fight by reasoning that the latter is a '*two-way thing where people are disagreeing so its two people doing something negative to each other*'. Overall, she presents a sound understanding of bullying.

When starting school, Samantha and her best friend engaged in bullying behaviours but by the end of Year 4 they had stopped. She explains that they encouraged each other and '*it was a bad relationship in that we bullied together*'. During this time they bullied children who were '*quieter than us and didn't have many friends and sort of a bit shy ... probably just different in any way I guess*'. During her early primary school years, Samantha continued to bully others but could not recall being reprimanded. As noted, Samantha's parents encouraged her to empathize with victims. Through this explicit approach, Samantha came to realize '*Oh this is how I have made people feel*', and this encouraged her to stop bullying. This empathy was absent in the case of both Rebecca (bully) and John (persistent bully). Samantha had never been victimized at school and, once she stopped bullying, she would actively intervene when others were bullied. According to Rigby and Johnson (2006), students are more likely to intervene if they show a positive attitude towards victims and believe that their parents would expect them to intervene.

In Samantha's eyes, home life is responsible for persistent bullying: '*home life is a big thing ... if the schools are doing all they can and they are putting in all these research strategies and it's still happening then it has to be the home or society*'. She suggests that persistent bullies may be victims at home by explaining:

> *I was picked on by my brother and my cousins and then my best friend had an older sister so I think she was probably picked on, so we sort of joined forces and we started picking on people maybe because we were picked on and we just thought that's what you do.*

To reduce persistent bullying, Samantha suggests that schools need to develop a cohesive ethos in which stakeholders are a community, a view that was also expressed by Abbie.

> *Making schools into real communities where parents feel that they are welcome ... and kids feel comfortable ... and that you feel like you're as one in the school ... okay we're a team here ... we need to work together rather than just individual classes, individual kids, because I think when you feel like you are part of something special you don't want to stuff it up ... you know you don't want to be the kid that is messing up the whole thing.*

A point of contrast between Samantha, who desisted, and Rebecca and John, who did not, was the ability to gain and maintain friendships. This and further contrasts are outlined in Table 1.

Factors that distinguish John from Samantha include rejection and the absence of any secure attachment. Possibly influenced by his lack of social skills, John found the experience of changing schools extremely difficult, whereas Samantha transitioned with ease. Her close relationships with parents, teachers and peers equipped her with confidence. Their positive perceptions of her verified her own self-view, setting up a positive cycle of behaviour and reinforcement, unlike John. By her own account, this was one reason why she ceased bullying others, yet upon deeper consideration other factors also appeared to protect Samantha from engaging in further bullying or becoming a victim.

TABLE 7.1 What sets Samantha, Rebecca and John apart?

Samantha desister	Rebecca bully	John persistent bully
Strong sense of belonging	No sense of belonging	No sense of belonging
Lifelong friends	Superficial friendships	No friends except one very short-lived relationship
Best friends	Her sister as her best friend and worst enemy	No best friend
Close, positive relationships with parents, extended family, teachers and peers	Lack of close relationships	No close relationships
Was viewed positively by parents and teachers	Negatively viewed by others	Negatively viewed by others
Demonstrated empathy	No apparent empathy	Highlights empathy as a problem
Views bullying negatively	Vilifies victims	Views bullying positively
Ability to self-regulate behaviour	Lacks ability to self-regulate and take responsibility for actions	Lacks ability to self-regulate

Risk factors and protective mechanisms

Desisters, like Samantha, are typically characterized as having low levels of aggression and anxiety and these may be the most robust of all protective mechanisms against victimization (Goldbaum, Craig, Pepler & Connolly 2008). While Samantha engaged in bullying with her best friend, it has also been recognized that the presence of a best friend can buffer against victimization or engaging in bullying behaviour (Bollmer, Milich, Harris & Maras 2005). This becomes particularly evident when comparing Samantha's lived experiences with those of Rebecca, Abbie and John. Samantha had a best friend from a very early age, yet John and Rebecca – and to a lesser extent Abbie – experienced peer rejection throughout most of their school life.

In a study of 10–13 year olds, Bollmer et al. (2005) found that

> children who displayed externalizing behaviours and had a higher quality best friendship were significantly less likely to engage in bullying behaviour than children displaying externalizing behaviours but who had a lower quality best friendship.

(p. 708)

High-quality friendships provide a template for healthy peer relationships and an environment for children to learn and practise the important social skills needed to develop positive peer relationships. For Samantha, these social skills were also emphasized in her home life, which further protected her from engaging in persistent bullying.

Samantha's parents discussed and modelled prosocial behaviour, encouraging her to reflect on her actions and the impact these had on others, and she believes this contributed to her ceasing to bully. In contrast, Abbie, John and Rebecca described parents who modelled and employed power to ensure that rules and routines were followed. It is well evidenced that parents who use power-based discipline as a means of increasing status in relation to their children are actually modelling these strategies to their children, who then transfer them to their own peer relationships (Baldry & Farrington 2000; Curtner-Smith 2000; Stevens, De Bourdeaudhuij & Van Oost 2002). Thus, by modelling these aggressive scripts, parents make behaviours such as bullying appear normal and influence their child's peer relationships (Huesmann 1988).

For Samantha, the relationships that she shared with her family, teachers and peers seemingly protected her from engaging in persistent bullying or becoming a victim.

Chapter summary

According to Pepler et al. (2008), desisters share a similar profile to those who have never engaged in bullying. Desisters, like Samantha, experience few problems with moral disengagement and aggression, and engage in low conflict with parents and peers and low levels of bullying. Samantha enjoys close relationships with family and peers, takes responsibility for her actions and attributes successes and failures internally where appropriate. She easily makes and maintains friends, sharing a number of long-term relationships.

Samantha engaged in bullying behaviours in her early years, but ceased once she matured. During these early years, Samantha bullied children she perceived as weaker and/or less popular than her. Believing that home life and society contribute to persistent bullying, she proposes that a cohesive school ethos and positive home and school relationships may reduce persistent bullying. Upon reflection, Samantha believes that her close, supportive family helped to change and end her bullying behaviour.

Chapter 8 will explore the lived experiences of those who are neither bullied nor bully. These bystanders represent the majority of the peer group, therefore gaining insight into their understandings is essential.

References

Baldry, A.C. & Farrington, D.P. (2000) Bullies and delinquents: Personal characteristics and parenting styles. *Journal of Community and Applied Social Psychology*, 10(1), pp. 17–31.

Bollmer, J.M., Milich, R., Harris, M.J. & Maras, M.A. (2005) A friend in need: The role of friendship quality as a protective factor in peer victimization and bullying. *Journal of Interpersonal Violence*, 20(6), pp. 701–712.

Coie, J.D. & Dodge, K.A. (1988) Multiple sources of data on social behaviour and social status in the school: a cross-age comparison. *Child Development*, 59(3), pp. 815–829.

Curtner-Smith, M.E. (2000) Mechanisms by which family processes contribute to school-age boys' bullying. *Child Study Journal*, 30(3), pp. 169–186.

Goldbaum, S., Craig, W.M., Pepler, D.J. & Connolly, J. (2008) Developmental trajectories of victimization. *Journal of Applied School Psychology*, 19(2), pp. 139–156.

Guerin, S. & Hennessey, E. (2002) Pupils' definitions of bullying. *European Journal of Psychology of Education*, 17(3), pp. 249–261.

Huesmann, L.R. (1988) An information processing model for the development of aggression. *Aggressive Behavior*, 14(1), pp. 13–24.

Pepler, D.J., Jiang, D., Craig, W.M. & Connolly, J. (2008) Developmental trajectories of bullying and associated factors. *Child Development*, 79(2), pp. 325–338.

Rigby, K. & Johnson, B. (2006) Expressed readiness of Australian schoolchildren to act as bystanders in support of children who are being bullied. *Educational Psychology*, 26(3), pp. 425–440.

Stevens, V., De Bourdeaudhuij, I. & Van Oost, P. (2002) Relationship of the family environment to children's involvement in bully/victim problems at school. *Journal of Youth and Adolescence*, 31(6), pp. 419–428.

8

BYSTANDERS

For my Year 11 prom we were out and I was with this girl. She is just like 'Oh can you hold my drink?' and I'm like 'okay' and I turned around and she was there and she actually bashed me and it was the worst experience ... I just remember being on the ground just like praying that it would stop and I'm there with so many people around watching.

(Brooke, 23 years old)

The voices of victims, bullies, bully/victims, desisters and persistent bullies have provided deeper insight into the phenomenon of persistent bullying. Yet what is missing are the voices of a significant population – those who stand by in bullying situations and ultimately decide whether to intervene, observe, reinforce or ignore. In Chapter 3, Brooke described her experiences of being persistently bullied. Her words, which open this chapter, highlight the powerful role that the group plays in bullying situations. In Chapters 8 and 9 we focus directly on sharing the voice of bystanders, and the role they play in face-to-face or online bullying. To begin, we hear from bystanders who directly observe bullying in face-to-face encounters.

Bullies are often motivated by status and dominance, therefore the peer group or audience plays an important role in determining who has the power within the group (Hawkins, Pepler & Craig 2001; Long & Pellegrini 2003; Sijtsema, Veenstra, Lindenberg & Salmivalli 2009). Bystanders' actions can actually enhance the bully's social status by 'spreading the word' among others that the bully is powerful. As evident in John's narrative, this reputation may act as a self-fulfilling prophecy (DeRosier, Cillessen, Coie & Dodge 1994). Also, the actions, or lack of action, of individuals or members in a group observing the bullying can be seen as supportive, reinforcing the bully's behaviour and increasing the likelihood of repetition.

Since the mid-to-late 1900s it has been recognized that children who are neither bullies nor victims are often present in bullying situations. Despite students reporting that they do not like bullying and are disgusted by the behaviour, many do not intervene (O'Connell, Pepler & Craig 1999). Therefore, self-awareness and an understanding of the roles that bystanders may take is essential. Bystanders can play active or non-active roles, with some indirectly or directly supporting either the victim or the bully, while others remain uninvolved. Salmivalli et al. (1996) explored various active and non-active roles that bystanders play. These are often influenced by an individual's emotions, attitudes and motivations and in turn provide members of the peer group with a sense of belonging. Some of the roles that bystanders may play include the *follower, reinforcer, outsider* and *defender*, with the most common being the latter three. It has been suggested that females are more likely to be defenders and outsiders, while males are generally reinforcers, however this gender difference is not supported by all studies.

Bystanders are more likely to intervene on behalf of the victim if they have done so before, are pro-victim, and hold the belief that others – particularly their friends – would expect them to intervene (McLaughlin, Arnold & Boyd 2005; Price et al. 2014). Nickerson, Mele and Princiotta (2008) found that feelings of empathy increased the likelihood of students acting as defenders or outsiders. However, others purport that empathy alone is not enough (Gini, Albiero, Benelli & Altoè 2008; Warden & Mackinnon 2003) and that the necessary skills to effectively intervene are also required (Gini et al. 2008). It is important to note, however, that when bystanders *do* intervene their actions are successful in the majority of instances (Rigby & Johnson 2006).

The following perspectives draw on self-reports of young people as well as reports from others including school leadership and school counsellors. We share the experiences of four bystanders: 'Trent' – defender; 'Zoe' – outsider; 'Rick' – outsider; and 'Ben' – follower.

The story of Trent, a defender

> *I've been here all my life since Reception so I know most of the bullying techniques.*
>
> (Trent, ten years old)

Defenders are students whose behaviour involves comforting or taking the side of the victim and attempting to stop bullying (Salmivalli 1999). These individuals typically have a higher self-esteem, productive coping strategies and are more altruistic and friendly than their peers (Tani, Greenman, Schneider & Fregoso 2003). It is therefore not surprising that peers rate defenders as being the most popular among their peer group (Salmivalli et al. 1996). Although earlier research found that defenders are typically female (Jeffrey, Miller & Linn 2001; Rigby & Johnson 2005), more recent research found that empathy rather than gender was a key factor (Nickerson, Mele & Princiotta 2008). We begin exploring the perspective of 'Trent' who, according to the Deputy Principal and School Counsellor, does not have a history of either bullying or victimization. Trent helps and supports the victim suggesting that he is a 'defender'.

Trent is a ten-year-old boy in Year 5 at an independent, co-educational Reception–Year 12 school located in Adelaide, South Australia. He has attended this school since Reception. Trent's parents and siblings mean a lot to him and he particularly values their support and cohesion in times of difficulty. One of his favourite pastimes outside of school involves spending time with his immediate and extended family. In difficult times, Trent initially turns to his mum but, like Samantha, he feels that he could rely on any member of his immediate or extended family for support. He appears to acknowledge and take responsibility for his behaviour and has a clear understanding of behavioural expectations and consequences. Trent engages in various sports and is a successful dancer, something he is proud of. His biggest regrets centre solely on not achieving good grades at school.

Trent presents as an articulate, confident and mature young boy who has the ability to view things optimistically. He demonstrates future aspirations and hopes to have a career in Science or Marine Biology. Trent describes himself positively and believes his teachers would say he is *'good … I bring happiness to the class, I bring good ideas … I'm well mannered'*.

Family and peer relationships

Trent enjoys a close relationship with all members of his family and is closest to his mum. In fact, research suggests that those who have a secure attachment to their mother are more likely to defend the victims of bullying (Lieberman, Doyle & Markewicz 1999; Nickerson, Mele & Princiotta 2008). Likewise, fathers play an important role and young people who share a secure attachment with their father, like Trent, are less likely to engage in bullying behaviour and more likely to act prosocially (Nickerson, Mele & Princiotta 2008). Trent also shares close, supportive relationships with other members of his immediate and extended family. Secure attachments provide children with a safe, trusting environment where they can communicate openly and ask for advice (Nickerson, Mele & Princiotta 2008) thus modelling the behaviours needed to act as a defender in bullying situations.

When Trent misbehaves, his parents discuss his behaviour with him prior to removing privileges such as having friends over, playing on the computer or watching television. Their parenting style can be classified as authoritative (Baumrind 1971). Students whose parents employ this authoritative approach to parenting are more psychosocially mature, more academically competent, less prone to internalize distress and less likely to engage in problem behaviours (Steinberg & Blatt–Eisengart 2006).

When asked about his popularity among peers, Trent responds *'I don't really care. I don't really bother'*. Despite this, he has four close male friends who, like him, are seldom reprimanded. Trent has experienced various emotional difficulties and therefore demonstrates understanding and empathy for those with similar challenges. When discussing a friend who experiences emotional issues, Trent explains that he '*doesn't know who he is picking on, he just picks on them … he hurts people sometimes he just gets really angry and walks off*'. Trent appears to be an understanding, empathetic young person, who is loyal to his friends. Empathy enables him to feel the pain of others, therefore when someone is being bullied he understands their hurt and has the confidence to intervene and support the victim (Nickerson, Mele & Princiotta 2008).

Trent's understandings and experiences of bullying and persistent bullying

Trent describes bullying as '*one kid being mean to a couple of others or one*'. He understands the role of power imbalance in bullying: '*they think they have power over other people*', and provides an example of one of his friend's little buddies being yelled at and pushed around by an older and stronger student. For Trent, bullying differs from a fight because '*bullying is when someone's picking on someone but through personal feelings and things … fighting is through different sorts of things*'. Throughout the conversation Trent refers to the emotional impact that bullying has on victims. Such feelings and experiences mirror the difficulties he has faced in his own life. He empathizes with victims saying that '*we're all different*' and believes that no one deserves to be bullied '*unless they've bullied before*'. This presents as an interesting and somewhat complex perception.

Trent's experiences as a defender provide a unique lens to consider persistent bullying. He describes a recent incident in which he and his friends actively intervened to help a Reception boy who was being bullied:

> One of them is bullying him so we're protecting the little kid by saying 'please stop being mean to him and pushing him around, yelling at him' … We say 'please step away from my friend's buddy' and then … just because my friend is about this high and his buddy is about this high, he fits perfectly on his back, so we just get him on a piggyback and run off so he doesn't bully him.

Neither Trent nor his friends reported this or other similar incidents to their teachers '*because … they'll work it out 'cause there's a whole bunch of Year 3s that are doing it so we won't just tell and we don't know all their names*'. In stating '*we don't know all their names*', Trent also appeared to deflect responsibility for reporting the incident. The bystander effect – in which the more people present, the less inclined they are to assist a person in distress – seemingly reduces the likelihood of reporting such incidents (Latané & Darley 1968). Furthermore, some reports have found that males are less likely to report incidents of bullying to teachers than females (McLaughlin, Arnold & Boyd 2005), a trend evident in this case.

Trent believes that students engage in persistent bullying because '*they're down through something that's happened in their life and they need to take it out on someone*' or they are '*being picked on at home … they have problems outside of school like their parents*' *could be really mean to them ... or abusive or stuff like that'*. Although Trent may be echoing his parents' understandings, he nonetheless believes that persistent bullies enter school and *'feel like they have to take the pressure out on someone else to stop it'*. Therefore, he suggests that schools need to take a proactive stance in understanding possible causes of persistent bullying while involving authorities like the police where necessary.

> *Try to figure out why they're bullying people and what's the problem with it, basically get inside their mind, emotions and things, sort of and work them out and then just go from there.*

Educating students about individual differences and diversity will, in Trent's eyes, also reduce persistent bullying. He explains that persistent bullies need to understand that *'we're all different so it doesn't matter if you pick on someone different 'cause you're different to them so then other people can pick on you, so it's basically everyone can pick on everyone'*. To reduce bullying, he suggests using a continuum of consequences ranging from detention to suspension or exclusion depending on the harm caused to the victim:

> *If they ... physically hurt someone then it deserves ... if they badly hurt them then it deserves ... suspension almost ... to expulsion if they hurt them emotionally and they're emotionally wrecked for the next three years ... well then they deserve expulsion, and if they ... just be mean well then maybe just detention.*

To gain further insight into bystander's understandings of bullying, each bystander participating in the research was presented with the hypothetical scenario of being knocked over while waiting in the canteen line. They were asked to comment on whether the act was perceived as intentional or not, and whether this would differ if the student were known to be a persistent bully. Trent demonstrated an 'attributional bias' (Dodge 1980; Dodge & Frame 1982) by interpreting the actions as intentional and wrong if perpetrated by a known bully, but accidental if the transgressor was not a known bully. Attributional bias refers to errors that people make when evaluating or trying to understand others' or their own behaviour.

Risk factors and protective mechanisms

Various factors present in Trent's life protected him from engaging in bullying or being victimized by others. Friends act as a buffer for both victimization and bullying (Shin 2010). Trent was relatively popular in his peer group and enjoyed a close friendship with four other males who shared similar prosocial attributes.

Close family relationships also protect children against bullying and victimization. Trent described a cohesive and loving immediate and extended family who were actively engaged in his life. For instance, Trent's grandma and two aunties went with him to a national dance competition. Their involvement in his life provided a protective buffer against bullying (Orpinas & Horne 2006). These close relationships not only model prosocial behaviours but provide Trent with a safe place if and when he faces challenges. He feels well supported and loved, which in turn protects him from bullying others and being bullied (Orpinas & Horne 2006).

Summary of Trent's perspective

Trent takes a proactive stance in terms of bullying, and is prepared to support and protect the victim. Trent demonstrates a high degree of empathy for others and a well-developed understanding of the emotional implications of bullying, often exhibiting maturity beyond his years. Close relationships with family and friends are important to Trent, and such relationships have seemingly protected him against bullying and victimization. Trent's narrative has provided insights into the life and perceptions of someone who is willing to defend victims. We now turn to the bystander role of 'outsider'.

The story of Zoe, an outsider

> *I feel that I should go help them and say 'Hey leave this person alone' but when I think of that I always think that I'm going to get bullied as well because I said that to them … so I don't do anything.*

(Zoe, eleven years old)

Like Trent, 'Zoe' was also identified by the Deputy Principal as neither bully nor victim. Despite her desire to help others, she does not actively intervene in bullying situations, fearing she may be the next victim. This is a view commonly expressed by primary school students (see McLaughlin, Arnold & Boyd 2005; Twemlow, Fonagy & Sacco 2004). Zoe describes behaviour that is consistent with an 'outsider': those students who stay away and do not take sides when bullying is happening (Salmivalli 1999). Tani and colleagues (2003) suggest that outsiders may have 'little or no concrete grasp of the extent to which victimized children suffer' (p. 142).

Zoe is an eleven-year-old female in Year 6 at a co-educational independent school in Adelaide, South Australia, which she has attended since Reception. Her proudest moment involves learning to ride a two-wheel bike. Zoe presents as articulate, friendly and honest, but appears to lack confidence at times. She is frequently reprimanded by teachers for asking multiple questions before commencing a task. Zoe views herself positively and believes others would say she *'helps people out if they're stuck on something'*.

Family and peer relationships

Zoe has a large extended family where she is the eldest child. However, unlike Trent, she does not feel close to any member of her immediate or extended family.

She lives with her mum, dad and younger brother and describes a family that appears to lack cohesion. Zoe is frequently yelled at by her parents and she is often unsure why. She finds her parents difficult to talk to and therefore turns to her teacher in times of trouble. As mentioned when discussing Trent's case, secure attachments with parents provide an opportunity to openly discuss challenging or threatening situations such as bullying, and predicts the likelihood of a student taking action to defend a victim (Laible & Thompson 2000; Nickerson, Mele & Princiotta 2008). Unfortunately, Zoe does not share this type of secure relationship with either parent and lacks opportunities to discuss situations and issues that are concerning for her. Consequently, she does not have the practice ground needed to learn how to defend others, and finds herself reluctant to support or defend victims at school.

Zoe regrets that her relationship with her brother is fraught with difficulties. While Zoe does not bully at school she identifies her actions towards her brother as bullying, something that she believes is acceptable because '*you love them in a kind of a way and they know that you won't mean it in every way because they're your sibling*'.

At home, discipline usually involves positive punishment, however negative reinforcement is employed at times, particularly when visitors are present. Zoe describes inconsistent house rules that leave her feeling unsure of expectations and consequences for misbehaviour. Although Zoe describes difficulties in her relationships at home, this is not the case at school where she shares positive relationships with her teachers and peers.

Zoe has four friends that she spends time with at recess and lunchtime. They usually go to the tennis courts or the oval and sit and talk; occasionally they play '*truth or dare*'. As two of the girls in the group '*like to be involved with boys*', their dares often involve boys; this is not the case for Zoe and the other two girls. These girls' behaviours are consistent with what Thorne and Luria (1986) term 'border work'; intense interactions involving the opposite gender through games such as chasey, truth and dare, and so forth. Zoe, from her own perspective, considers herself to be reasonably popular among her peers. Her understandings of bullying provide insights from an outsider's perspective.

Zoe's understandings and experiences of bullying and persistent bullying

Zoe understands bullying as '*a person .... says something and they start teasing them or hurting them for no reason or just for fun for themselves 'cause they might think it's fun but other people don't*'. She also believes that bullying needs to be an intentional physical act that causes harm, yet does not believe that indirect acts constitute bullying.

> *If you're using contact with each other then I think it* [is] *more a bit more bullying ... I think I describe a fight as being very loud and angry with the other person.*

For Zoe, a fight involves more overt anger than bullying. She also believes that you cannot bully your friends because you can 'make up' with each other; that is, she does not believe that a bully and victim can '*make up unless the teacher made you*'. She views bullies as '*mean and horrible and that they should understand that you shouldn't bully 'cause if someone did it to you how would you feel?*' Zoe presents two conflicting views when asked whether victims deserve to be bullied. Initially she proposed that they deserve to be bullied because of their difference, yet, once the conversation focused solely on bullying her response changed to '*no I don't think so*'. The latter response may have been influenced by a desire to present herself in a favourable light or because the word 'bullying' was used, which was absent in earlier discussions (Arora & Thompson 1987).

Despite her own outsider response to bullying, Zoe believes that bystanders should intervene and seek the help of a teacher if they witness bullying. When presented with the hypothetical canteen scenario discussed previously, Zoe demonstrated an attributional bias whereby she immediately perceived the known bully's actions to be deliberate.

> *Because they're bullies and they just do it for, you know, their reason is to be a bully and they like being a bully.*

Like John, Zoe proposes that some students persistently bully to provide fun for themselves and others, which enhances their identity, reputation and status in the peer group:

> *Just for fun 'cause they might think it's fun … because other people might see them do it and think that they're really tough or popular or cool.*

Sadly, although Zoe believes that her teachers do everything possible to reduce bullying, she does not think that schools can stop the behaviour: '*I don't think there is anything that we could do*'.

Risk factors and protective mechanisms

When unpacking Zoe's narrative, a number of risks are evident. Zoe describes a family that lacks cohesion and closeness which potentially places her at risk of bullying, as either bully or victim (Orpinas & Horne 2006). Her parent's authoritarian parenting style, which often involves punishment, places her at further risk (Ladd 1992). Zoe perceives the rules, boundaries and consequences as inconsistent and harsh. There is little or no communication between herself and her parents which appears to be mitigated by the protective mechanism of the close relationships that she shares with her teachers (Green, Oswald & Spears 2007; Österman 2000). She feels that she can turn to them in difficult times and they will support and help her. Protective factors that buffer against bullying behaviour or victimization include social competence and sound relationships with her teachers (Orpinas & Horne

2006). Despite this, Zoe lacks the confidence to intervene and defend victims and instead remains on the outer so that she avoids being the next victim.

Summary of Zoe's perspective

Zoe presented as a reserved young lady who is articulate yet lacks confidence in her academic abilities at school. Her family life appears somewhat disjointed and her parents employ both negative and positive punishment as part of their authoritarian parenting style. Her relationship with her brother is turbulent. At school, Zoe enjoys positive relationships with her teachers and a small group of close friends. She understands that bullying is an intentional act that causes harm. Zoe, like Trent, demonstrates an attribution bias where she believed that known bullies are in the wrong even when their actions may be innocent. These attributions are concerning as they will influence the way that she behaves and treats these students. Despite her caring nature and desire to help victims of bullying, Zoe fears being the next victim and therefore does not actively intervene. We turn now to another outsider, Rick, whose stance, unlike Zoe, is underpinned by past experiences of victimization.

The story of Rick, another outsider

> At my old school in Portugal there was this big boy. He got suspended in the whole year twelve times … he broke a kid's arm and the kid's leg … he started pushing me around when I was playing and then he just started swearing and then I went to tell and he got suspended and then it happened too many times and they expelled him.
>
> (Rick, eleven years old)

Although 'Rick' was bullied in his home country, Portugal, he has not engaged in bullying nor has he been victimized since arriving in Australia. He does not actively support bullies but neither does he intervene in most cases, suggesting that he is a bystander who takes on the role of outsider.

Rick is an eleven-year-old boy in Year 6 at an independent co-educational Reception–Year 12 school in Adelaide, South Australia. He migrated from Portugal with his family approximately two years ago. He presents as an honest, confident and articulate young man who volunteered information with little prompting. Rick is active and athletic; he loves sport, particularly tennis and soccer. He aspires to be a professional tennis player. Rick believes his teachers would describe him as 'good, but sometimes like when he's around his friends he goes out of task sometimes just a bit … I don't like to be mean to other people – I don't do that'. He feels that his parents would describe him as 'good mannered and … a bit lazy – a lot lazy'.

Rick's proudest moments both in and out of school centred on achievements such as receiving 'straight A's last year' and various sporting trophies. His biggest regret involved not being able to compete at Sports Day because of an ankle injury. Rick is empathetic towards victims of bullying and demonstrates compassion for his teacher when others are disruptive or misbehaving:

> I feel sorry for the teacher 'cause he might make him feel like that he's not explaining … that his stuff is boring and he's not paying attention to the teacher so the teacher might feel pretty bad.

Family and peer relationships

Rick is part of a family of five; mum, dad, an older and younger sister. He describes a close cohesive family whose members support each other and enjoy spending time together. He proudly announced each family member's birth date, illustrating an interest and connection with them. In contrast to Zoe, Rick enjoys a close relationship with his sisters and is often found '*playing with them … we like to play together*'. His parents appear consistent with their discipline, providing clear expectations. They employ negative punishment as part of their authoritative parenting style. He describes his parents as supportive, particularly during times of trouble. For instance, when he was bullied in Portugal his parents supported him and he is confident they would do so again if necessary. He therefore has no hesitation in turning to them, as he believes they will help to resolve issues concerning him. Rick's parents also encourage autonomy by encouraging him and his older sister '*to visit Portugal in not these holidays but the next … and stay at my grandparent's house*'. This supportive family environment has provided Rick with the necessary social skills to develop positive peer relationships.

Rick describes himself as being relatively popular and belongs to what he classifies as the '*popular group*'. Rick identifies five best friends and a group of thirty others with whom he associates. Rick also remains in contact with his friends in Portugal, affirming his ability to gain and maintain friendships. Despite communicating regularly with his friends in Portugal, Rick misses them a lot and is looking forward to spending time with them when he returns for a holiday. Although Rick's home life is significantly different from Zoe's, he also acts as an outsider in bullying situations.

Rick's understandings and experiences of bullying and persistent bullying

For Rick, bullying involves '*a kid like much bigger and not your age, like a bit older than you, like going up to you and starts swearing at you, like pushing you around and teasing you*'. He believes bullying differs from a fight as the former is one-sided. Rick describes victims as '*really weak or something; maybe they look small maybe they look scared*', highlighting a power imbalance. He describes some of the direct forms of bullying typically observed among males, such as '*swearing, teasing and pushing them to the ground*' (Olweus 1993; Smith 2004). Rick's understandings were underpinned by his own experiences of bullying.

Although Rick is no longer bullied, he was victimized earlier in his school life, making him reluctant to intervene when others are bullied. Having said this, Rick describes an incident where he had the confidence to walk away from those who bully.

> *Well I had a friend that bullied people, then I just didn't want to be his friend anymore 'cause if I kept on being his friend he'd probably drag me into the bullying thing, but then I just stopped playing with him and made new friends.*

He suggests that bystanders should report bullying to a teacher if they are in a group, however, if they are alone he believes they should ignore the situation to avoid being victimized, a view also expressed by Zoe. Identifying the actions of a known bully to be deliberate, Rick, like other bystanders, demonstrates an attributional bias when presented with the hypothetical canteen scenario outlined previously. Rick believes a lack of monitoring and discipline at home may underpin persistent bullying, supporting Pepler et al.'s (2008) findings.

> *I think it would just be maybe the family's fault 'cause ... they don't ground them or something; I'm not sure.*

In Rick's eyes, lacking the feeling of belonging may also contribute to persistent bullying: '*they don't have any friends and they feel bad*'. He suggests that the need to gain acceptance may motivate and reinforce persistent bullying, as was evident in John's narrative. To address persistent bullying, Rick recommends excluding these students from '*lunch or recess for a week*' and if this fails, schools should suspend or expel them. This view is concerning because, while exclusion, suspension and expulsion may reduce bullying temporarily, these approaches do little to address the root causes of the problem or increase school safety in the long term (Skiba & Peterson 1999). In fact, in some cases, suspension and/or exclusion reinforce aggressive behaviour, triggering a perpetual cycle (Tobin, Sugai & Colvin 1996). If bullying is considered a relationship problem as Pepler (2006) suggests, then exclusion fails to provide the necessary relationship solutions.

Friendships are important to Rick who describes himself as '*more popular ... 'cause I hang out with people who do lots of stuff so they're popular, I hang out with them*'. Despite the importance that he places on friendships, severing ties with a friend who had started to bully shows that Rick is confident in establishing new relationships.

Risk factors and protective mechanisms

Although Rick was previously bullied, he has a number of protective mechanisms that would work to buffer against victimization. For instance, he is part of a close, warm and loving family environment where his parents employ an authoritative parenting style and encourage autonomy. He also has a close group of friends who support him and fulfil his sense of belonging. Rick's achievements in sport have also acted as a buffer against bullying and victimization.

Summary of Rick's perspective

Rick comes from a close family and is a confident and articulate young man who volunteered information with little or no probing, suggesting that he is open and honest. Rick has a positive sense of self in terms of his sporting achievement and abilities:

> *So I'm representing, I'm going to try and represent South Australia in like, and like play New South Wales 'n Victoria and all those … I'm going on the, like, higher one so I'm versing other states not schools.*

His desire to be active is reflected in his attitude to schoolwork; he likes subjects that keep him busy and engaged. Rick consistently referred to his dreams and aspirations, illustrating a futures perspective which can act as a buffer to help him cope with adversities in life as and when they arise. Rick is also quite popular among his peers and has a number of close friends as well as a larger peer group that he socializes with. He appears to have a positive identity, including high self-esteem and a sense of purpose in his life. Rick is empathetic towards others and demonstrated compassion when discussing his feelings towards his teacher when others in the class were disruptive and misbehaving. Having considered the lived experiences of bystanders who defend and those who are outsiders, it is now pertinent to consider the narrative of a follower.

The story of Ben, a follower

> *I just do what they do 'cause then they might end up not being friends with me.*
> (Ben, 10 years old)

Like Rick, friends mean everything to 'Ben', however, in contrast to Rick, he is prepared to support friends who bully, and only intervenes if this will not jeopardize his friendships. At times, Ben's bystander behaviour is consistent with that of a 'follower' who supports the bully without participating; at other times he appears to play an 'assistant' role by actually assisting the bully and joining in (Salmivalli et al. 1996).

Ben, a ten-year-old boy in Year 5 at a co-educational independent Reception–Year 12 school in Adelaide, South Australia, presents as a confident young person who does not take responsibility for his actions. Instead he deflects the focus onto something or someone else. When discussing misdemeanours, Ben quickly diverts the focus onto something more positive. He has high expectations of himself and is disappointed when he receives low grades at school or cannot complete something he starts. Ben's favourite pastime involves socializing with friends and his proudest moments centre on helping or interacting with others as opposed to solo achievements.

Family and peer relationships

Ben was reluctant to discuss his family – mum, dad and younger sister. When probed, he describes a secure attachment with both parents, being closest to his mum and enjoying spending time with his dad as the water boy for his football team. Ben describes himself in a positive light by saying that he is helpful, a view he believes his parents would share. He is not close to his sister whom he fights with often.

Ben considers himself reasonably popular at school. He is often easily led and will act in a manner that impresses his peers or gains their support. The following provides just one of many examples:

> I like to make people join in and help people that have no one to play with maybe, and they wanted to play one particular game maybe if my friends would agree well we'll do that.

Evidently, the group dynamics at any given time will either positively or negatively determine Ben's behaviour. Thus, if his group of friends believe that bullying is unacceptable then Ben will not bully, yet if they decide that it is acceptable then he is likely to engage in bullying, a description supported by the school counsellor. Ben's understandings of bullying are also underpinned by his need to belong and be liked by his peers.

> People shouldn't tease them and then you'd have more friends. 'Cause if you're teasing someone that has a couple of friends that you want to be friends with, you wouldn't probably pick on the person with the friends that you want to be with 'cause then if you do that the person that's getting teased won't, um the two other people maybe won't want to be friends with you.

Ben's understandings and experiences of bullying and persistent bullying

Ben understands bullying to involve

> people saying 'No you can't play' and then people saying 'Tell your friends you can have a chip' and then someone that you don't like comes up and says that and then you say no and then people just not letting other people play.

Although Ben could not distinguish between bullying and a fight, he understands that bullying is repetitive. He spoke consistently about bullying and teasing interchangeably, suggesting that for him, they are the same concept, a view evidenced in other studies (e.g. Cross et al. 2009). In his eyes, bullying is a normal part of growing up and occurs because the bully and victim do not get along, supporting Pepler's (2006) view that bullying centres on relationships. Ben, like Trent, refers to individual difference which can result in some students being victimized: '*they're different and don't like each other and, or the person doesn't like them*'. He believes that victims who '*haven't got any friends to help them*' do not deserve to be bullied, yet others do '*sometimes, maybe*'. If victimized, Ben would walk away and later disclose the bullying to his parents, actions he suggests others should follow.

Unlike the other bystanders in this study, Ben has engaged in low level bullying. Twelve months before our conversation he joined and supported a bully to avoid jeopardizing their friendship. Ben's discussion of bullying centred solely on friendships and relationships, possibly because they were so important to him.

Ben, like John, identifies boredom as underpinning and reinforcing persistent bullying: '*they think it's something to do instead of just doing something boring – something to do so they want to keep on doing it*'. Like other primary school students, Ben identified teachers and education as key elements in reducing persistent bullying (McLaughlin, Arnold & Boyd 2005). Ben's suggestions included focusing on peer relationships and explicitly teaching persistent bullies about the impact of their behaviour.

Despite the importance he placed on friendships, Ben recommends that schools should exclude persistent bullies. Similar to the other bystanders in this study, he exhibited an attributional bias when presented with the hypothetical scenario.

Risk and protective factors

In Ben's case the relationship that he has with his peers can be considered both a risk and a protective factor for bullying. On the one hand, he could engage in bullying if his peer group were to do so. But on the other hand, given that friends can buffer against bullying (Shin 2010), they could protect him from being victimized or engaging in further bullying. If his peer group acts prosocially there is every possibility that Ben will follow suit.

Having a secure attachment to his parents also protects Ben against bullying and victimization. In particular, sharing a secure relationship with his father means that Ben is less likely to engage in bullying behaviour and more likely to act in a prosocial manner (Nickerson, Mele & Princiotta 2008).

Although both risks and protective mechanisms are evident in Ben's life, it would appear that, at this stage in his life, his peers hold the key. Therefore it is important to recognize the importance of peer relationships and the role they may play in determining whether a child, like Ben, is victimized or engages in bullying.

Summary of Ben's perspective

Ben did not appear to be as confident or articulate as the other bystanders we have discussed. He seemed apprehensive and a little reserved at first, but once discussions turned to his proudest moments and his sport he opened up. Ben is creative and has a high level of self-efficacy when it comes to his schoolwork. He holds high expectations of himself and is a high achiever. Ben is a very social young person who values his friendships, however he is also easily influenced by his friends and what they think. According to the Deputy Principal and Counsellor, Ben's involvement in bullying was his way of maintaining his status within the peer group.

What influences bystanders' decisions to act or not?

Historically, bullying has been identified as primarily a group phenomenon which plays out in the presence of the peer group (Salmivalli et al. 1996). Bystanders are present in 85 per cent to 88 per cent of childhood bullying incidents (Atlas & Pepler 1998) and can respond either positively or negatively. Positive bystander behaviour, some of which was evident in Trent's case, includes defending the victim, reporting the incident to adults, challenging the bully's power and/or status (Salmivalli 2010) and – the most common – comforting or giving advice to the victim (DeSmet et al. 2016). Negative bystander behaviour, which was evident in Ben's narrative, includes joining, assisting and reinforcing the bully's behaviour or passively looking on (Salmivalli 2010). If bystanders intervene, the bullying stops within ten seconds in 57 per cent of cases. So their action is potentially powerful and can yield a quick resolution. Yet often young people do not intervene (Dillon & Bushman 2015; Shultz, Heilman & Hart 2014).

Being a close friend is the strongest predictor of whether a person will display positive bystander behaviours (Price & Green 2016; Price et al. 2014). In order to intervene, students also need a high level of self-efficacy and the appropriate skills and attitudes, including a belief that they can make a difference, positive attitudes about intervening and negative attitudes about passively standing by (DeSmet et al. 2016). Individuals are also more likely to display positive bystander behaviours if, like Rick, they have been victimized themselves or, like Trent, they are empathetic towards the victim and believe they are not at fault (DeSmet et al. 2016; Machackova, Dedkova, Sevcikova & Černá 2015). For others, like Ben, bystander behaviour is underpinned by the belief that their friendships, popularity and status will increase by supporting or reinforcing the bully; therefore they are unlikely to act in a prosocial way. As Ben describes '*I just do what they do 'cause then they might end up not being friends with me*'.

Chapter summary

Bystanders' understandings of bullying are important in determining whether or not they intervene. While each bystander in this chapter recognized bullying as an intentional act, their understanding of power and repetition varied. Both Trent and Rick focused on power in terms of size or age, with Rick explaining that the degree of power increased the victim's fear. Although Naylor, Cowie, Cossin, de Bettencourt and Lemme (2006) suggest that male students are more likely than females to identify repetition as a component of bullying, Ben was the only male in this group to do so. Ben and Zoe concentrated on the act itself. The impact of bullying also featured in the bystanders' definitions. For Ben, this component, together with repetition, distinguished bullying from a fight. In his eyes, if the outcome was '*bad*' then it was bullying, if not, then it was teasing. Trent spoke exclusively about the emotional impact of bullying on victims. His views support those who reason that victims' interpretations are important when determining whether an act qualifies as bullying (or teasing) (see Pawluk 1989; Shapiro, Baumeister & Kessler 1991; Vessey, Duffy, O'Sullivan & Swanson 2003). Strategies employed by bullies were also included in these bystanders' definitions, with Ben identifying teasing as the most harmful form of bullying, a finding consistent with Cross et al. (2009).

Past experiences have shaped bystanders' behaviour and level of empathy towards victims and bullies. Each of the bystanders demonstrated empathy towards victims, peers, teachers or siblings, contrasting with the bullies. Nickerson, Mele and Princiotta (2008) found that empathy increases the likelihood of students acting as defenders or outsiders; however, it has been suggested that empathy alone may not be enough (Gini et al. 2008; Warden & Mackinnon 2003). For students to effectively intervene they also need high levels of social self-efficacy (Gini et al. 2008). Both empathy and self-efficacy were evident in Trent's case, whereas Rick empathized with victims but lacked the skills to intervene. Clark and Ladd (2000) found that an individual's degree of empathy was linked to the number and quality of their friends, indicating that students like Rick who have a large number of friends would be more empathetic than peers with few or no friends.

When discussing the possible reasons for persistent bullying, participants identified a number of influential factors including families, parenting styles, lack of consequences, victimization, home life, lack of friends and social status. Providing entertainment for themselves or others, needing to be accepted and enhancing one's identity were also identified by the bystanders as motivating and reinforcing persistent bullying (Olthof & Goossens 2008; Pepler 2006). An interplay between these elements is suggested as a student might persistently bully to provide 'fun' and 'enjoyment' for others, which may in turn help to meet their need to be accepted while also enhancing their identity and reputation.

Each bystander demonstrated an attributional bias when provided with the hypothetical scenario, highlighting their belief that the actions of a known persistent bully would be intentional, while the actions of other peers would be considered accidental. These attributions impact on students' responses and behaviours, even if they are erroneous (Snyder, Tanke & Berschield 1977). By interpreting the act as intentional these bystanders may be hostile and act in self-defence, possibly escalating the situation. Attributions and perceptions also influence the way that persistent bullies are perceived and treated, further influencing the bullies' behaviour and setting up a perpetual cycle (refer to Chapter 6 for a more detailed discussion).

Although many bystanders in this chapter were reluctant to intervene, their suggestions to reduce persistent bullying centred on involving teachers in bullying incidents, supporting the views of researchers (e.g. McLaughlin, Arnold & Boyd 2005; Rogers & Tisak 1996). Unless bullying is reported to them or they witness it themselves, teachers are unaware of the bullying and cannot respond (Pepler & Craig 1995; Rigby & Johnson 2006). Trent suggested a range of strategies to reduce persistent bullying in schools, including attempting to understand bullies and their individual circumstances, adopting an individualized approach, and supporting and providing assistance to offenders. He further suggested using a continuum of punishment, where first offenders are treated more leniently than persistent bullies. On the other hand, Zoe thought that there was little that schools could do to reduce or stop the behaviour.

Chapter 8 has presented the voice of bystanders who play various roles in incidents of face-to-face bullying. However, with the increasing presence of technology in young people's lives, the use of online platforms to victimize has taken centre stage in many discussions of bullying. Chapter 9 will therefore present the voice and experiences of the 'hybrid' bystander who navigates both face-to-face and online environments.

References

Arora, C.M.J. & Thompson, D.A. (1987) Defining bullying for a secondary school. *Educational and Child Psychology*, 4(3/4), pp. 110–120.

Atlas, R.S. & Pepler, D.J. (1998) Observations of bullying in the classroom. *Journal of Educational Research*, 92(2), pp. 86–98.

Baumrind, D. (1971) Current patterns of parental authority. *Developmental Psychology Monograph*, 4(2), pp. 1–103.

Clark, K.E. & Ladd, G.W. (2000) Connectedness and autonomy support in parent–child relationships: Links to children's socioemotional orientation and peer relationships. *Developmental Psychology*, 36(4), pp. 485–498.

Cross, D., Shaw, T., Hearn, L., Epstein, M., Monks, H., Lester, L. & Thomas, L. (2009) *Australian covert bullying prevalence study (ACBPS)*. Perth: Edith Cowan University Child Promotion Research Centre.

DeRosier, M.E., Cillessen, A.H.N., Coie, J.D. & Dodge, K.A. (1994) Group social context and children's aggressive behavior. *Child Development*, 65(4), pp. 1068–1079.

DeSmet, A., Bastiaensens, S., Van Cleemput, K., Poels, K., Vandebosch, H., Cardon, G. & De Bourdeaudhuij, I. (2016) Deciding whether to look after them, to like it, or leave it: A multidimensional analysis of predictors of positive and negative bystander behavior in cyberbullying among adolescents. *Computers in Human Behavior*, 57, pp. 398–415.

Dillon, K.P. & Bushman, B.J. (2015) Unresponsive or un-noticed?: Cyberbystander intervention in an experimental cyberbullying context. *Computers in Human Behavior*, 45, pp. 144–150.

Dodge, K.A. (1980) Social cognition and children's aggressive behavior. *Child Development*, 51(1), pp. 162–170.

Dodge, K.A. & Frame, C.L. (1982) Social cognitive biases and deficits in aggressive boys. *Child Development*, 53(3), pp. 620–635.

Gini, G., Albiero, P., Benelli, B. & Altoè, G. (2008) Determinants of adolescents' active defending and passive bystanding behavior in bullying. *Journal of Adolescence*, 31(1), pp. 93–105.

Green, D.M., Oswald, M. & Spears, B. (2007) Teachers' (mis)understandings of resilience. *International Education Journal*, 8(2), pp. 133–144.

Hawkins, D.L., Pepler, D.J. & Craig, W.M. (2001) Naturalistic observations of peer interventions in bullying. *Social Development*, 10(4), pp. 512–527.

Jeffrey, L.R., Miller, D. & Linn, M. (2001) Middle school bullying as a context for the development of passive observers to the victimization of others. *Journal of Emotional Abuse*, 2, pp. 143–156.

Ladd, G.W. (1992) Themes and theories: Perspectives on processes in family–peer relationships. In R.D. Park & G.W. Ladd (eds), *Family-peer relationships: Modes of linkage*. Hillsdale, NJ: Erlbaum, pp. 3–34.

Laible, D.L. & Thompson, R.A. (2000) Mother-child discourse, attachment security, shared positive affect and early conscience development. *Child Development*, 71, pp. 1424–1440.

Latané, B. & Darley, J.M. (1968). Group inhibition of bystander intervention in emergencies. *Journal of Personality and Social Psychology*, 10(3), p. 215–221.

Lieberman, M., Doyle, A.B. & Markewicz, D. (1999) Developmental patterns in security of attachment to mother and father in late childhood and early adolescence: Associations with peer relations. *Child Development*, 70, pp. 202–203.

Long, J.D. & Pellegrini, A.D. (2003) Studying change in dominance and bullying with linear mixed models. *School Psychology Review*, 32(3), pp. 401–417.

Machackova, H., Dedkova, L., Sevcikova, A. & Černá, A. (2015) Empathic responses by cyberbystanders: The importance of proximity. *Journal of Youth Studies*, pp. 1–12. DOI: 10.1080/13676261.2015.1112882.

McLaughlin, C., Arnold, R. & Boyd, E. (2005) Bystanders in schools: What do they do and what do they think? Factors influencing the behaviour of English students as bystanders. *Pastoral Care in Education*, 23(2), pp. 17–22.

Naylor, P., Cowie, H., Cossin, F., de Bettencourt, R. & Lemme, F. (2006) Teachers' and pupils' definitions of bullying. *Journal of Educational Psychology*, 76(3), pp. 553–576.

Nickerson, A.B., Mele, D. & Princiotta, D. (2008) Attachment and empathy as predictors of roles as defenders or outsiders in bullying interactions. *Journal of School Psychology*, 46(6), pp. 687–703.

O'Connell, P., Pepler, D.J. & Craig, W.M. (1999) Peer involvement in bullying: Insights and challenges for intervention. *Journal of Adolescence*, 22(4), pp. 437–452.

Olthof, T. & Goossens, F.A. (2008) Bullying and the need to belong: Early adolescents' bullying-related behavior and the acceptance they desire and receive from particular classmates. *Social Development*, 17(1), pp. 24–46.

Olweus, D. (1993) *Bullying at school: What we know and what we can do*. Oxford: Blackwell.

Orpinas, P. & Horne, A.M. (2006) *Bullying prevention: Creating a positive school climate and developing social competence*. Washington, DC: American Psychological Association.

Österman, K.F. (2000) Students' need for belonging in the school community. *Review of Educational Research*, 70(3), pp. 323–367.

Pawluk, C.J. (1989) Social construction of teasing. *Journal for the Theory of Social Behavior*, 19(2), pp. 145–167.

Pepler, D.J. (2006) Bullying interventions: A binocular perspective. *Canadian Journal of Child Adolescent Psychiatry*, 15(1), pp. 16–20.

Pepler, D.J. & Craig, W.M. (1995) A peek behind the fence: Naturalistic observations of aggressive children with remote audio-visual recording. *Developmental Psychology*, 31(4), pp. 547–553.

Pepler, D.J., Jiang, D., Craig, W.M. & Connolly, J. (2008) Developmental trajectories of bullying and associated factors. *Child Development*, 79(2), pp. 325–338.

Price, D. & Green, D.M. (2016) Power of peer relations in determining cyber-bystander behavior. In M.F. Wright (ed), *A social-ecological approach to cyberbullying*. New York, NY: Nova Science Publishers, pp. 181–196.

Price, D., Green, D.M., Spears, B., Scrimgeour, M., Barnes, A., Geer, R. & Johnson, B. (2014) A qualitative exploration of cyber-bystanders and moral engagement. *Australian Journal of Guidance and Counselling*, 24(1), pp. 1–17.

Rigby, K. & Johnson, B. (2005) Student bystanders in Australian schools. *Pastoral Care in Education*, 23(2), pp. 10–16.

Rigby, K. & Johnson, B. (2006) Expressed readiness of Australian schoolchildren to act as bystanders in support of children who are being bullied. *Educational Psychology*, 26(3), pp. 425–440.

Rogers, M.J. & Tisak, M.S. (1996) Children's reasoning about responses to peer aggression: Victim's and witness's expected and prescribed behaviors. *Aggressive Behavior*, 22(4), pp. 259–269.

Salmivalli, C. (1999) Participant role approach to school bullying: Implications for interventions. *Journal of Adolescence*, 22(4), pp. 453–459.

Salmivalli, C. (2010) Bullying and the peer group: A review. *Aggression and Violent Behavior*, 15(2), pp. 112–120.

Salmivalli, C., Lagerspetz, K.M.J., Björkqvist, K., Österman, K. & Kaukiainen, A. (1996) Bullying as a group process: Participant roles and their relations to social status within the group. *Aggressive Behavior*, 22(1), pp. 1–15.

Shapiro, J.P., Baumeister, R.F. & Kessler, J.W. (1991) A three component model of children's teasing: Aggression, humor, and ambiguity. *Journal of Social and Clinical Psychology*, 10(4), pp. 459–472.

Shin, Y. (2010) Psychosocial and friendship characteristics of bully/victim subgroups in Korean primary school children. *School Psychology International*, 31(4), pp. 372–388.

Shultz, E., Heilman, R. & Hart, K.J. (2014) Cyber-bullying: An exploration of bystander behavior and motivation. *Cyberpsychology: Journal of Psychosocial Research on Cyberspace*, 8(4), doi: 10.5817/CP2014-4-3.

Sijtsema, J.J., Veenstra, R., Lindenberg, S. & Salmivalli, C. (2009) Empirical test of bullies' status goals: assessing direct goals, aggression, and prestige. *Aggressive Behavior*, 35(1), pp. 57–67.

Skiba, R.J. & Peterson, R. (1999) The dark side of zero tolerance: Can punishment lead to safe schools? *Phi Delta Kappan*, 80(5), pp. 372–382.

Smith, P.K. (2004) Bullying: Recent developments. *Child and Adolescent Mental Health*, 9(3), pp. 98–103.

Snyder, M., Tanke, E.D. & Berschield, E. (1977) Social perception and interpersonal behaviour: On the self-fulfilling nature of social stereotypes. *Journal of Personality and Social Psychology*, 35(9), pp. 656–666.

Steinberg, L. & Blatt-Eisengart, I. (2006) Patterns of competence and adjustment among adolescents from authoritative, authoritarian, indulgent and neglectful homes: A replication in a sample of serious juvenile offenders. *Journal of Research on Adolescence*, 16(1), pp. 47–58.

Tani, F., Greenman, P.S., Schneider, B.H. & Fregoso, M. (2003) Bullying and the Big Five: A study of childhood personality and participant roles in bullying incidents. *School Psychology International*, 24(2), pp. 131–146.

Thorne, B. & Luria, Z. (1986) Sexuality and gender in children's daily worlds. *Social Problems*, 33, pp. 176–190.

Tobin, T., Sugai, G. & Colvin, G. (1996) Patterns in middle school discipline records. *Journal of Emotional and Behavioral Disorders*, 4(2), pp. 82–94.

Twemlow, S.W., Fonagy, P.F. & Sacco, F.C. (2004) The role of the bystander in the social architecture of bullying and violence in schools and communities. *Annals of the New York Academy of Sciences*, 1036(1), pp. 215–232.

Vessey, J., Duffy, M., O'Sullivan, P. & Swanson, M. (2003) Assessing teasing in school-age youth. *Issues in Comprehensive Pediatric Nursing*, 26(1), pp. 1–11.

Warden, D. & Mackinnon, S. (2003) Prosocial children, bullies and victims: An investigation of their sociometric status, empathy and social problem-solving strategies. *British Journal of Developmental Psychology*, 21(3), pp. 367–385

9

CYBER AND HYBRID BYSTANDERS

There is the internet as well ... and that is worse ... at least in the old days you bullied at school and then you went home and you slept it off.

(Abbie, 23 years old)

Abbie, who we met in Chapter 4, explains how much worse her experiences with bullying would have been had they occurred online. In Chapter 8, we shared the perceptions of those who played various bystander roles in face-to-face bullying. Chapter 9 specifically focuses on the role of online bystanders in cyberbullying and how their action, inaction, decisions, attitudes, and inter-relationships with the bully or victim influence their behaviour. Given the explosion of digital technologies and everyday communication via online platforms, the phenomenon of bullying has unfortunately traversed into this realm. In the lives of young people, everyday activities occur across both face-to-face and online environments. Therefore, it is essential to equip them with the necessary skills to be safe and support others to be safe in both environments. This chapter begins by distinguishing between face-to-face and cyberbullying then focuses on the cyberbystander and the newly coined term of a 'hybrid' bystander who moves between face-to-face and online environments (Price et al. 2014).

To gain greater insight into the phenomenon of cyberbullying and bystander responses, a digital animation was produced by a professional animator. The animation shows the silhouettes of two teens fighting, watched by a row of bystanders; a scenario which regrettably occurs frequently in schoolyard altercations. One of the fighters is depicted as larger than the other and bystanders are presented in baggy clothes to ensure that they appear gender-neutral. One of the bystanders has a mobile phone which they use to view and record the fight. The scenario ends with the send button being hit and the video being shared and uploaded to YouTube. For the purposes of the research, 961 South Australian secondary school students

(Years 8–12, average age of 15 years) viewed the animation and were asked to identify potential bystanders and individuals who they perceived were able to help the victim.

To understand the role of bystanders in this scenario, we first need to consider more closely the similarities and differences between face-to-face and cyberbullying, and the impact that each may have on victims and bystanders.

What are the differences between face-to-face and cyberbullying?

With the ubiquitous use of technology for communication, it has not taken long for online bullying among young people to become a concern. Researchers have found a relationship between face-to-face and cyberbullying; students who bully or are victimized face-to-face are more likely to bully or be victimized online (Li 2007; Mishna, Khoury-Kassabri, Gadalla & Daciuk 2012). In fact, engaging in face-to-face bullying is one of the strongest predictors of cyberbullying engagement (Sticca, Ruggieri, Alsaker & Perren 2013).

As was the case in the animation, bullying often originates in the school ground during school hours but continues after hours online (Spears, Slee, Owens & Johnson 2009). Movement from the offline environment to an online setting and back again suggests a cyclic relationship between both contexts (Spears et al. 2009). While this may be the case, the majority of cyberbullying occurs outside of school hours and is less frequent than face-to-face bullying, yet has a larger impact on its victims (Smith, Mahdavi, Carvalho, Fisher, Russell & Tippett 2008). As suggested by Abbie at the outset of this chapter, in cases of cyberbullying, victims gain no reprieve by going home; instead they report feeling targeted 24 hours a day, 7 days a week. The anonymity of cyberbullying adds to its detrimental impact on the victim (Nixon 2014), and increases the level of fear (Bauman 2010). Half of the victims in Slonje and Smith's (2008) study did not tell anyone about the cyberbullying, which further increased its impact. Up until recently, the 'digital divide' between young people and their parents resulted in most victims choosing to remain silent, rather than turning to adults for help (Dooley, Gradinger, Strohmeier, Cross & Spiel 2010; Smith et al. 2008); and even when they did report, not much changed (Davis & Nixon 2013).

Those who engage in cyberbullying exhibit low self-esteem, difficulties with peer and family relationships, decreased empathy, and the tendency to trivialize their bullying behaviour. John, our persistent bully, shared many of these characteristics, suggesting that, had he been at school today, he may have become involved in cyberbullying others (Bonanno & Hymel 2013; Campbell et al. 2012; Olenik-Shemesh, Heiman & Eden 2012). Given that face-to-face bullying is a potential stepping stone for cyberbullying, there is a need for schools and the broader community to address and reduce the more traditional form of bullying, as this may create a positive ripple effect for online bullying. We suggest that one of the most successful approaches involves empowering bystanders.

When is an act like the fight considered bullying?

When does a scenario like the fight presented earlier in this chapter become bullying? We decided to ask our secondary school students. For many of them, once the fight started it was considered bullying as '*someone was getting punched*'; however, for others, the act of uploading the incident to YouTube but not necessarily sending it to friends or others signified that it was bullying.

> *I know guys, a lot of them just fight for the hell of it, but if someone is filming it to show others, I believe THAT is when it becomes bullying.*

Yet no one identified the actual act of viewing and then sending the video to others as bullying; that is, only *viewing* the material was considered bullying. This is surprising and concerning because schools have been trying to educate students about the dangers of cyberbullying and one would have expected that today's students would be very aware of the impact on the victim of forwarding such material.

To determine when the fight was considered bullying by the research participants, we used the following three constructs: repetition, power imbalance and impact on the victim. We discuss each in turn.

Repetition

The inclusion of repetition in definitions of face-to-face and cyberbullying is contentious, with some academics believing that it is crucial (Farrington & Ttofi 2009; Olweus 1993), while others disagree (Guerin & Hennessey 2002; Terry 1998). Yet, in the eyes of young people, the repetitive and ongoing nature of bullying is more harmful than an isolated act. The secondary school students who viewed our fight scenario used similar descriptions to those of Leah (a victim) and Rebecca (who self-identified as a bully) when describing bullying.

> *Bullying is doing bad things to a person more than one time and the film got sent to everyone on YouTube which is pretty much the whole world.*

The ongoing and repetitive nature of bullying contributes to the power imbalance between the bully and victim.

Power imbalance

In face-to-face bullying a power imbalance can be manifested in a number of ways: size, age, number of perpetrators, image and status, to name a few. These themes were discussed in Chapter 1. Similar themes of power emerged from the online fight scenario. Some secondary students merely acknowledged the existence of a power imbalance by saying that it was bullying because '*someone was hurting someone who had less power*'. Others pinpointed power by describing the group of bystanders as '*a mob of people was bullying the one person*'. Interestingly, the animation did not intend to show a power imbalance, therefore these views represent the unsolicited interpretations of young people.

Impact on the victim

Like Brooke and Abbie, who were both victims of bullying, the young people surveyed used the impact on the victim to qualify the incident as either bullying or fighting. Many secondary school students who viewed the scenario identified the incident as bullying because '*it causes harm to the victim*'. Others considered the impact once the video was online, saying '*recording it and then probably laughing is bullying because one or more of them might have got seriously hurt*'. We challenge you to consider: if students identify the incident as bullying by the negative impact on the victim, why don't they intervene?

What influences cyberbystanders' decisions to act or not?

In Chapter 8, we discussed the various roles that bystanders play in face-to-face bullying. In the fight scenario presented earlier, bystanders are those who '*can stop the people filming it and hopefully stop a domino effect. If the fight isn't stopped at least the video evidence could be*'. But what role do they play online? Like face-to-face bullying, bystanders are present in the majority of cyberbullying situations, however the anonymity of the online environment creates challenges as often the perpetrator and bystander(s) do not witness the victim's distress. Cyberbystanders are more likely to experience an empathetic response if they are present when the incident occurred or are informed by the victim, yet whether they intervene or not is largely based on 'directness' and 'proximity' (Machackova et al. 2015, p. 8). This is nothing new as Latané and Darley, as far back as 1968, wrote about the *bystander effect* whereby bystanders only act when they: notice the situation; recognize that the person needs assistance; feel personally responsible; believe they are able to help and then consciously decide to act. All of these factors require the bystander to have some contact with the victim and be within close proximity of the incident. Similar studies have considered the bystander effect online and found that the quickest response occurs when the victim actually requests help (Blair, Foster Thompson & Wuensch 2005; Markey 2000). This has immediate implications for anti-bullying education as victims often do not ask for help or report bullying, therefore they need the vocabulary and confidence to do so. In line with the bystander effect however, some of our secondary students reported being less likely to intervene if '*they thought that they were the only ones that would intervene and they did not want to get laughed at*'. For others, the decision not to intervene centred on protecting their image or viewing the bully as cool and powerful. Consequently, bystanders often report being afraid to intervene explaining that '*they were scared that maybe someone would bash them up for interfering*'.

The relationship shared with the victim also directly affects whether a bystander will intervene. If the victim is a friend, the chances of a bystander intervening are greater (Price & Green 2016). High school students explain that '*if your mate was in a fight you would help him and stand by them*'. When the same cohort of students viewed a Facebook de-friending scenario they believed that they should intervene '*because they are friends*' (Price & Green 2016). Being friends, either face-to-face or online, implies certain responsibilities that include trying '*to intervene to stop them getting injured*'. Unfortunately, as we saw in Brooke's case, the victim's friends often lack the skills to intervene and, like Zoe, some support the bully as they fear being attacked themselves (Green 2015; Salmivalli, Huttunen & Lagerspetz 1997). As Zoe described,

> *I feel that I should go help them and say 'Hey leave this person alone' but when I think of that I always think that I'm going to get bullied as well because I said that to them … so I don't do anything.*

Providing bystanders with effective language and opportunities to practise intervening safely is needed. However, one questions whether online intervention requires a different skill set to intervention recommended for addressing face-to-face bullying.

In relation to the digital animation presented at the outset of this chapter, most students identified bystanders as those watching the fight, filming it, receiving the footage and/or watching it on YouTube. Bystanders watching the fight were perceived to be in the best position to help and the most likely to intervene because '*as a whole they could have stopped the fight*'. Those filming the fight were acknowledged as being able to help by simply not recording or uploading the incident. Once the footage was uploaded, students believed that bystanders should report the incident to authorities, delete it or refrain from forwarding it to others. Those in authority were considered more likely to intervene '*because they are less likely to be influenced by the atmosphere and feeling of being present at the fight – not scared by people who may turn on them if trying to speak up at the fight*'. Many students acknowledged that it was right or moral to intervene in the bullying scenario, and also in the Facebook de-friending scenario mentioned previously (Price & Green 2016). Those physically present at the fight were considered to be in the ideal position to intervene because those '*that aren't actually at the fight can do little to stop it*'. There was a perceived shift in responsibility once the incident went online '*because they are not caught up in the shock of seeing a fight in real life, they would feel more detached from the scenario and feel easier to report it*'. The idea that the responsibility to intervene applies only if bystanders are physically present is quite challenging in terms of addressing cyberbullying and empowering cyberbystanders.

Anonymity of the victim, bully and bystander is another factor that seemingly influences bystanders' behaviour online, as their ability to make a sound decision about intervening is challenged if they do not witness the victim's distress. In the case of the fight scenario it is possible that the victim's distress was evident, however in other acts of cyberbullying this is not the case. This further increases the negative impact on victims, as they often feel isolated and lonely (DeSmet et al. 2016; Fox & Moreland 2015). In terms of the fight scenario, secondary school students were divided in their opinion of how anonymity influenced an online bystander's behaviour. Some suggested that viewing the fight scenario online provided protection to the bystander as they were unaware of who the victim/s or bully/ies were and would therefore be more inclined to intervene. Other students recognized that with anonymity came a displaced or removed responsibility which influenced their decision to intervene. Acknowledging that '*no one else was*' intervening seemingly also influenced a bystander's behaviour to intervene or not to intervene, suggesting that peer influence is also a factor that determines altruistic behaviour.

Further, identifying that intervening '*is the right thing to do*' and that bystanders should intervene '*because it* [fighting] *is obviously a stupid thing to do and shouldn't be done*' and '*they know it is the wrong thing to do*' (Price & Green 2016) was also seen as underpinning decisions to intervene or not. '*Because fighting is wrong … publicly broadcasting it is also wrong as it humiliates the victim as anyone can see it*'. Perceptions such as this, indicates that one should intervene because of the impact of a potentially global audience. These comments suggest that bystanders use their moral judgement to determine whether or not to act.

Rather than seeing the negative impact of the fight, many students described the incident as *fun*, which led to their justification that no intervention was needed. Unfortunately, the notion of fun often arises when students talk about bullying (Green 2015), as was evidenced in the earlier narratives of Leah, John and Zoe. If students see such acts as harmless and fun then they will be unlikely to intervene, particularly if the behaviour is reinforced by the peer group. Reinforcement can involve '*people cheering them on and telling them to bash each other up*'. This reaffirms that adequate education about bullying behaviours should be central to any intervention. Such education may need to distinguish more clearly between fun and bullying while highlighting what is acceptable in relationships and what is not.

The secondary students also identified a 'hybrid' bystander, one who initiated bullying offline yet became a bystander in the online environment (Price et al. 2014). We suggest that this new form of bystander is a lynchpin between the offline and online environment (Price et al. 2014). Other studies have found that once online, bystanders switch and begin to bully, possibly because of a reduced sense of responsibility and increased sense of anonymity (Barlińska, Szuster & Winiewski 2013). This was highlighted in our fight scenario '*because the first attack initiated the bullying, with bystanders and filming the fight*'. In this instance the bully instigated the fight in a face-to-face setting yet watched the impact on the victim unfold in an online environment. This person therefore played two roles – bully and bystander – and each role negatively impacts on the victim. So not only is it important to understand the decision-making processes of bystanders, it is also necessary to address the emerging role of the hybrid bystander, who is both bully and bystander.

Chapter summary

Unfortunately, as the use of technology increases, so does the number of cyberbullying incidents. This form of bullying has an extremely detrimental effect on victims. Using a digital animation of a fight as a prompt, secondary students provided insight into factors that may influence their decisions on whether or not to intervene. Being present when an act of aggression occurs had a significant impact on whether bystanders felt morally obligated to intervene or not. The anonymous nature of the online world means that bullies and bystanders do not see first-hand the impact that bullying is having on victims, therefore they feel less inclined to intervene. While anonymity seemingly prevents online bystanders from intervening it can also buffer and reduce the fear that often paralyses face-to-face bystanders and stops them intervening.

There is an urgent need to ensure that young people acquire the necessary skills to be safe both in face-to-face and online environments, as seamless movement between both settings is now a natural and everyday activity. Importantly, young people need to be empowered to intervene confidently when they witness any form of bullying, including cyberbullying. The voices reflecting multiple perspectives on persistent bullying have been shared in Parts II, III and IV, and highlight the impact, attitudes and behaviours associated with this phenomenon. In Part V, these voices underpin our discussion of educational policies, practices and proactive approaches to address the harmful behaviour of persistent bullying. We challenge the reader to think through and apply the suggestions advocated by these multiple first-hand perspectives, as everyone plays a role and can potentially have a significant impact on reducing bullying.

References

Barlińska, J., Szuster, A. & Winiewski, M. (2013) Cyberbullying among adolescent bystanders: Role of the communication medium, form of violence, and empathy. *Journal of Community & Applied Social Psychology*, 23(1), pp. 37–51.

Bauman, S. (2010) Cyberbullying in a rural intermediate school: An exploratory study. *The Journal of Early Adolescence*, 30(6), pp. 803–833.

Blair, C.A., Foster Thompson, L. & Wuensch, K.L. (2005) Electronic helping behavior: The virtual presence of others makes a difference. *Basic and Applied Social Psychology*, 27(2), pp. 171–178.

Bonanno, R.A. & Hymel, S. (2013) Cyber bullying and internalizing difficulties: Above and beyond the impact of traditional forms of bullying. *Journal of Youth and Adolescence*, 42(5), pp. 685–697.

Campbell, M., Spears, B., Slee, P., Butler, D. & Kift, S. (2012) Victims' perceptions of traditional and cyberbullying, and the psychosocial correlates of their victimisation. *Emotional and Behavioural Difficulties*, 17(3–4), pp. 389–401.

Davis, S. & Nixon, C.L. (2013) *Youth Voice project: Student insights into bullying and peer mistreatment*. Champaign, IL: Research Press Publishers.

DeSmet, A., Bastiaensens, S., Van Cleemput, K., Poels, K., Vandebosch, H., Cardon, G. & De Bourdeaudhuij, I. (2016) Deciding whether to look after them, to like it, or leave it: A multidimensional analysis of predictors of positive and negative bystander behavior in cyberbullying among adolescents. *Computers in Human Behavior*, 57, pp. 398–415.

Dooley, J.J., Gradinger, P., Strohmeier, D., Cross, D. & Spiel, C. (2010) Cyber-victimisation: The association between help-seeking behaviours and self-reported emotional symptoms in Australia and Austria. *Australian Journal of Guidance and Counselling*, 20(2), pp. 194–209.

Farrington, D.P. & Ttofi, M.M. (2009) Reducing school bullying: evidence-based implications for policy. *Crime and Justice*, 38(1), pp. 281–345.

Fox, J. & Moreland, J.J. (2015) The dark side of social networking sites: An exploration of the relational and psychological stressors associated with Facebook use and affordances. *Computers in Human Behavior*, 45, pp. 168–176.

Green, D.M. (2015) An investigation of persistent bullying at school: Multiple perspectives of a complex social phenomenon. Doctoral dissertation, University of South Australia.

Guerin, S. & Hennessey, E. (2002) Pupils' definitions of bullying. *European Journal of Psychology of Education*, 17(3), pp. 249–261.

Latané, B. & Darley, J.M. (1968) Group inhibition of bystander intervention in emergencies, *Journal of Personality and Social Psychology*, 10(3), pp. 215–221.

Li, Q. (2007) New bottle but old wine: A research of cyberbullying in schools. *Computers in Human Behavior*, 23(4), pp. 1777–1791.

Machackova, H., Dedkova, L., Sevcikova, A. & Černá, A. (2015) Empathic responses by cyberbystanders: The importance of proximity. *Journal of Youth Studies*, pp. 1–12.

Markey, P.M. (2000) Bystander intervention in computer-mediated communication. *Computers in Human Behavior*, 16(2), pp. 183–188.

Mishna, F., Khoury-Kassabri, M., Gadalla, T. & Daciuk, J. (2012) Risk factors for involvement in cyber bullying: Victims, bullies and bully-victims. *Children and Youth Services Review*, 34(1), pp. 63–70.

Nixon, C.L. (2014) Current perspectives: The impact of cyberbullying on adolescent health. *Adolescent Health, Medicine and Therapeutics*, 5, pp. 143–158.

Olenik-Shemesh, D., Heiman, T. & Eden, S. (2012) Cyberbullying victimisation in adolescence: Relationships with loneliness and depressive mood. *Emotional and Behavioural Difficulties*, 17(3–4), pp. 361–374.

Olweus, D. (1993) *Bullying at school: What we know and what we can do*. Oxford: Blackwell.

Price, D. & Green, D.M. (2016) Power of peer relations in determining cyber-bystander behavior. In M.F. Wright (ed), *A social-ecological approach to cyberbullying*. New York, NY: Nova Science Publishers, pp. 181–196.

Price, D., Green, D.M., Spears, B., Scrimgeour, M., Barnes, A., Geer, R. & Johnson, B. (2014) A qualitative exploration of cyber-bystanders and moral engagement. *Australian Journal of Guidance and Counselling*, 24(1), pp. 1–17.

Salmivalli, C., Huttunen, A. & Lagerspetz, K.M.J. (1997) Peer networks and bullying in schools. *Scandinavian Journal of Psychology*, 38(4), pp. 305–312.

Slonje, R. & Smith, P.K. (2008) Cyberbullying: Another main type of bullying? *Scandinavian Journal of Psychology*, 49(2), pp. 147–154.

Smith, P.K., Mahdavi, J., Carvalho, M., Fisher, S., Russell, S. & Tippett, N. (2008) Cyberbullying: Its nature and impact in secondary school pupils. *Journal of Child Psychology & Psychiatry*, 49(4), pp. 376–385.

Spears, B., Slee, P., Owens, L. & Johnson, B. (2009) Behind the scenes and screens: Insights into the human dimension of covert and cyberbullying. *Journal of Psyhology*, 217(4), pp. 189–196.

Sticca, F., Ruggieri, S., Alsaker, F. & Perren, S. (2013) Longitudinal risk factors for cyberbullying in adolescence. *Journal of Community & Applied Social Psychology*, 23(1), pp. 52–67.

Terry, A.A. (1998) Teachers as targets of bullying by their pupils: A study to investigate incidence. *British Journal of Educational Psychology*, 68(2), pp. 255–268.

PART V

Addressing the problem

10

RELATIONSHIPS, WELLBEING AND BULLYING

Multiple Perspectives in Persistent Bullying: Capturing and listening to young people's voices concludes in Part V by synthesizing the voices of the young people presented in previous chapters to make meaning and address the phenomenon of persistent bullying. To begin, Chapter 10 considers the important role that relationships play in persistent bullying and its impact on student wellbeing. This is followed in Chapter 11 by highlighting critical turning points and chain reactions in the lives of those who bully, are victimized or desist, which inform the educational implications presented in Chapter 12. As illustrated consistently through the voices of young people, persistent bullying requires immediate attention to improve the wellbeing of all stakeholders, and central to this is the desire to feel connected and to develop productive relationships with family, peers and teachers. However, relationships are influenced by the complex interplay between a range of factors including self-concept, status, self-verification, reputation enhancement, self-fulfilling prophecy, empathy and the need to belong. A sustained body of educational research has identified relationships as a key factor in the academic achievement and wellbeing of students, however we begin this chapter by emphasizing the pivotal role of relationships in addressing persistent bullying.

The pivotal role of relationships

As mentioned in Chapter 1, the need to belong is paramount for young people and they strive to fulfil this need immediately after meeting basic needs such as food and safety (Baumeister & Leary 1995; Maslow 1954). Belonging, whether to a peer group, family or community, involves relationships that are being continually negotiated and adjusted. Relationships play an important role in either motivating and reinforcing or buffering against persistent bullying. Status, identity and the need to belong were identified by John as key motivators for his own persistent bullying, consistent with research in this field (Burns, Maycock, Cross & Brown 2008). Bullies identified as high on Pepler et al.'s (2008) bullying trajectory demonstrated elevated risks in the parental and peer relationship domains, displaying significant problems early in their relationships. Positive relationships have been noted in those who are prosocial and/or desist bullying (Pepler, personal communication 2012), and appeared to be missing in Rebecca and John's lives. Secure parental and peer relationships are recognized protective mechanisms that can act as a buffer against engaging in bullying or being victimized (Orpinas & Horne 2006; Updegraff, Madden-Derdich, Estrada, Sales & Leonard 2002).

The foundations for positive relationships seemingly originate at home. Relationships with parents and siblings provide a training ground for early social skills. If these relationships are fraught with difficulties, opportunities for modelling and reinforcing positive social skills are missed. The situation is further exacerbated if the child has no friends as the environment to learn and practise the necessary social skills to develop social competence is lacking, subsequently resulting in a cycle of perpetual rejection (Dodge et al. 2003; Ladd 1999). Positive connections within the educational setting are vital as they influence student engagement, participation, academic achievement, completion rates, prosocial behaviours, health–risk behaviours, and teacher–student and peer relationships (Noble, McGrath, Wyatt, Carbines & Robb 2008; Price & McCallum 2016).

Relationships were paramount to all the young people whose voices have been shared in this book. For some, relationship difficulties led to being victimized; for others, the need to belong and be accepted underpinned bullying behaviour. Having identified the importance of relationships across multiple perspectives, we support the notion that bullying needs to be considered as a relationship problem. As highlighted, differences and similarities exist in the quality and quantity of relationships across all areas of these young people's lives. We now consider in turn the influence of family relationships, student–teacher relationships and peer relations.

Family relationships

Families play an important role in providing the necessary preparation for entry into larger social environments by modelling, reinforcing and directly or indirectly teaching members how to socialize. As noted, families provide the first social environment in which children learn the knowledge, competencies, attitudes and values necessary to effectively function throughout life. The likelihood of a child being bullied or engaging in bullying has been linked to different parenting styles, family values and cohesiveness (Bowers, Smith & Binney 1994; Smith, Bowers, Binney & Cowie 1993). Attachment style alone plays a role in influencing the behaviour of bullies, victims and bystanders (Nickerson, Mele & Princiotta 2008; Troy & Sroufe 1987). While an interplay between a child and their parent's temperament, parenting style and behaviour is noted, we focus on participants' perceptions of parenting and attachment styles. Further exploration is needed to determine the interplay between the other constructs.

Family relationships varied among the young people's experiences with some describing close relationships and secure attachments to their parents, and others recounting insecure attachments and dysfunctional relationships. The importance each individual placed on these relationships was evidenced either by the way they spoke, or the frequency with which they referred to family. For some, like Trent and Leah, family provided support during difficult times and a safe base from which they could learn, experiment and develop. For Brooke, Abbie and John, family relationships were associated with feelings of difference and alienation, possibly contributing to their peer relationship difficulties. Their parents often attributed blame for bullying or being bullied to their child.

Difficult family relationships, similar to those described by Brooke, can place females in particular at more risk of being victimized than their peers (Rigby 1994). Positive father–child relationships have also been noted for their critical role in reducing victimization (Nickerson, Mele & Princiotta 2008). Both Leah and Brooke lacked secure attachments to a father figure, placing them at further risk of being victimized. Having an overprotective mother increased Leah's risk of being victimized (Bowers, Smith & Binney 1994; Loeber & Dishion 1984; Orpinas & Horne 2006). These individuals experienced multi-layered risks in their family relationships.

Further risk factors for victimization were also evident in both Leah and Brooke's lives. For Brooke, these factors included decreased opportunities to socialize with peers, acting as the primary carer for her brother, feeling unsupported by her mother who held her responsible for being bullied, and lacking a secure attachment with either parent, all increased her risk of being victimized (Orpinas & Horne 2006; Stevens, De Bourdeaudhuij & Van Oost 2002). In contrast to Brooke, Leah described a secure attachment to her mother; however, this did not appear to protect her from being victimized, suggesting that more than one protective mechanism is needed. Nevertheless this relationship provided her with the confidence to disclose what was happening and to take actions to improve her situation. Secure attachments, particularly with parents or caregivers, cannot be understated as these early bonds shape internal representations of the environment, influencing future social experiences (Thompson & Raikes 2003). Those with a secure attachment are more likely to defend victims (Nickerson, Mele & Princiotta 2008) while those who experience an insecure attachment may develop a negative bias in their social interactions whereby they negatively misinterpret others' actions, making them more likely to bully or be bullied (Walden & Beran 2010).

Negative perceptions of families and parents have been noted among bullies (Cenkseven Onder & Yurtal 2008) and were consistently highlighted in the narratives of John and Rebecca, both of whom self-identified as bullies. Given that persistent bullies continue their behaviour in spite of interventions employed by schools, identifying differences between those who desist and those who persist may shed light on strategies to reduce bullying. One such difference is the way that parents model and manage behaviour. Samantha (a desister) was raised by parents who discussed and modelled prosocial behaviour, encouraging her to reflect on her actions and their impact on others, and she believes this contributed to her ceasing to bully (Nickerson, Mele & Princiotta 2008). In contrast, John, and to a lesser degree Rebecca, described parents who modelled and employed power to ensure rules and routines were followed. It is well evidenced that parents who use power-based discipline model these strategies to their children as a means of increasing their status among peers and the community (Baldry & Farrington 1999, 2000). This parenting style makes power-based behaviours such as bullying appear normal. By modelling these aggressive scripts, parent behaviours influence their child's later peer relationships (Huesmann 1988). Considering the significant role that parents play in socializing their children, John's parents inadvertently reinforced his bullying behaviour by modelling aggressive scripts.

The development of self-concepts is influenced by parental beliefs (Gecas & Schwalbe 1983). Parents often adopt a 'positivity' bias whereby they view their own child more positively than other children (Larrance & Twentyman 1983). While this was the case for most of the young people in this book, it was not so for John or Rebecca. As a teacher, John's mother was particularly aware of his misdemeanours at school and of other teachers' perceptions, and she grew to expect him to misbehave. This seemingly shaped John's behaviour, both at school and at home, having an impact on their relationship and reinforcing the negative dimensions of his behaviour.

Parents have a significant influence, particularly in the early years, but as children reach school-age their social world broadens. It is not surprising that the relationships between students and their teachers can become influential, given the amount of time they spend together.

Student–teacher relationships

Teachers are socialization agents, with student–teacher relationships having a powerful influence on children's social development (Davis 2003). They can help develop students' sense of belonging (Noddings 1988; Österman 2000) and social identity (Wentzel 1997). Positive student–teacher relationships can act as a buffer for students who, like Brooke, are at risk of being victimized (Green, Oswald & Spears 2007; Österman 2000). Research evidence therefore suggests that improving relationships between students and teachers may help to reduce bullying (Craig & Pepler 2007; Murray-Harvey & Slee 2010; Pepler 2006). Additionally, healthy relationships have reciprocal benefits, whereby teachers with a high level of wellbeing promote the wellbeing of their students, and vice versa (McCallum & Price 2010). Students who share positive relationships with their teachers are more likely to intervene in bullying incidents (Flaspohler, Elfstrom, Vanderzee, Sink & Birchmeier 2009). Student–teacher relationships are therefore powerful and may shed light on possible factors at the school level that either reinforce or reduce persistent bullying.

The young people in this book highlighted the powerful role that teachers can play in supporting students. However, in Brooke and Abbie's eyes, their teachers appeared to reinforce bullying at school. Abbie believed that her teachers had favourite students who could misbehave, and even bully, with few or no consequences. At school, both Brooke and Abbie were often made to feel responsible for being victimized and were therefore removed from areas where the bully was known to frequent. This left them feeling isolated and powerless while also sending the message that they were the ones who needed to make changes, rather than the bully. As a result, the power imbalance between the bully and victim increased, the bully's reputation was enhanced, and neither Brooke nor Abbie reported subsequent instances of victimization to school staff. John also described teachers' behaviours and attitudes that seemingly reinforced his persistent bullying. Their negative view of him had a detrimental effect on his social identity and self-concept, providing a reputation that he subsequently strived to fulfil.

The relationship between teacher and bully, as well as teacher and victim, governs how teachers respond and where they attribute blame. Teachers who view bullies favourably are more likely to assign blame to the victim (Nesdale & Pickering 2006), as evident in Brooke and Abbie's explanations. Furthermore, bullies who are popular students may be less likely to be reprimanded by teachers for their behaviour (Nesdale & Pickering 2006). A lack of action by teachers sends a clear message to peers that bullying is acceptable, thus decreasing future disclosures (Pepler, personal communication 2012; Unnever & Cornell 2004).

It is well recognized that high levels of connectedness with teachers can buffer against bullying and can positively affect academic achievement (Konishi, Hymel, Zumbo & Li 2010), therefore a greater focus on developing positive student–teacher relationships and an inclusive school climate may play a role in efforts to reduce persistent bullying.

Peer relationships

While healthy friendships offer many benefits for young people, rejection can lead to various emotional difficulties such as anxiety, depression, grief, isolation and loneliness (Baumeister & Leary 1995; Österman 2000). Peer rejection appeared to play an important role in the lives of both the bullies and victims described in this book. Unlike the bystanders (Trent, Zoe, Rick and Ben) and the desister (Samantha), Leah (a victim), Rebecca (a bully) and John (a persistent bully) struggled to gain and maintain friendships. Changing schools highlighted a further difference; Samantha transitioned with ease, whereas Leah and John found transitions extremely difficult, possibly influenced by limited social skills. Leah, Rebecca and John's perspectives suggested they lacked the necessary social skills to make and maintain quality friendships (e.g. effective conflict management strategies, group entry skills), possibly contributing to their victimization and bullying behaviour (Schneider, Atkinson & Tardif 2001; Szewczyk-Sokolowski, Bost & Wainwright 2005).

A lack of belonging has been found to lead to anti-social behaviours, such as bullying (Baumeister & Leary 1995). John explicitly described how his bullying behaviour was motivated and reinforced by his need to gain acceptance and recognition among his peers, viewing some attention as better than none. John's recollections of his early school days, where he went to quite extreme lengths to make connections, demonstrated his intense need to interact with peers. As he progressed through school, peers laughed at John's antics, further shaping his behaviour. A strong need to belong followed John throughout his school life. The use of power and status to escape loneliness and to gain a sense of belonging has been noted in the lives of bullies (Baumeister & Leary 1995; Juvonen, Graham & Schuster 2003). We suggest that John's behaviour may have been different had he established a strong sense of belonging. Alternatively, a best friend may have provided a 'template' for positive peer relationships, potentially changing his trajectory (Bollmer et al. 2005). Instead, he persistently bullied to meet his social goals of acceptance and status (Burns et al. 2008; Eslea et al. 2004). For John, bullying had adaptive benefits, making it unlikely that he would stop (Ellis et al. 2012).

The link between empathy and relationships

Relationships provide a reciprocal training ground for learning social skills. John appeared to lack many such skills including empathy, a characteristic that differentiated him from others in this book. The development of empathy helps individuals learn right from wrong, enabling them to develop social competence and meaningful relationships. Lacking the necessary social skills to gain and maintain friendships, John did not appear to have the training ground to learn to feel empathy, adding to his relationship problems and ineffective conflict management skills (de Wied, Branje & Meeus 2007), a trend also evident in Rebecca's case.

It is important to note that individuals who demonstrate high levels of empathy are less likely to harm others (Cohen & Strayer 1996). Empathy can motivate individuals to cease bullying as they become aware of the suffering they have caused (Kowalski, Giumetti, Schroeder & Lattanner 2014). It has consistently been found that bullies lack empathy (Feshbach 1975; Gini 2006; Olweus 1991). However, it is contended that instead of lacking empathy, bullies simply *choose* not to empathize (Sutton, Smith & Sweetham 1999). This was not the case with John, who described genuine concern for his victim *once* his teacher had explicitly explained the harm he had caused. However, John was unable to empathize with his other victims, or develop such understandings independently, suggesting a limited 'theory of mind' capacity. A theory of mind is crucial for empathy as it enables an individual to interpret and understand others' thoughts, feelings and intentions (Premack & Woodruff 1978). Although John had a strong desire to belong and to enhance his identity, his reduced cognitive ability to empathize with others contributed to further rejection and persistent bullying of others.

Through sharing John's perspective, questions have been raised that need further exploration. For instance, is empathy merely a matter of choice (Sutton, Smith & Sweetham 1999) or is something more at play? Could early intervention, social skills training and opportunities to practise new skills in a safe, inclusive environment help persistent bullies, like John, achieve their social goals in a more prosocial manner? If persistent bullies are unable to detect others' pain without being explicitly taught or alerted to such effects, then existing strategies to manage their behaviour may need to be reconsidered.

Persistent bullying, the need to belong and status

It has been suggested that popular students acquire a 'positive halo' that influences how others perceive, evaluate and respond to their behaviour (Hymel, Wagner & Butler 1990). In contrast, students who are rejected by their peers acquire a 'negative halo'. For John, belonging, along with status and identity – whether positive or negative – were central concerns. In his eyes, bullying helped to meet his social goals (i.e. belonging) and was therefore adaptive (Carroll, Hattie, Durkin & Houghton 2001; Ellis et al. 2012). Interventions and consequences employed by his school(s) inadvertently enhanced his identity and status. He became known as a 'bully' and 'trouble', labels that even today appear entrenched in his thinking and self-concept. John soon began acting in accordance with this reputation, further reinforcing his behaviour. When considering the theories of reciprocal determinism, self-verification and reputation enhancement (Bandura 1973; Emler 1984; North & Swann 2009), it is not surprising that John engaged in persistent bullying and that interventions appeared unsuccessful. Self-verification is underpinned by the belief that self-views provide an individual with a sense of coherence and an ability to predict and control their world (North & Swann 2009). Individuals actively seek information that validates or is consistent with their self-view. Therefore, given the link between an individual's sense of belonging and wellbeing, it is posited that whole-school approaches to promoting positive school ecology (Price & McCallum 2016) are vital if persistent bullying is to be disrupted.

The role of parent and teacher attitudes in bullying and victimization

As evidenced in the narratives in earlier chapters, parent and teacher attitudes can influence the behaviour and self-concept of both bullies and their victims. Often, students who persistently bully become recognized for their behaviour and develop a negative profile among parents, teachers and other school staff. Parents' and teachers' expectations can lead to self-fulfilling prophecies, reinforcing a student's behaviour and informing his or her self-beliefs and self-concept (Rosenthal & Jacobson 1968). When all parties hold a similar negative opinion, self-fulfilling prophecies are all the more powerful (Madon et al. 2001). John considered himself 'trouble', a view shared by his parents and the school community, and this became self-fulfilling.

At school, teachers can influence, either positively or negatively, a student's status within the peer group (Chan 2003). Teachers' expectations, beliefs and interactions shape the way that students perceive and treat their peers, shaping their self-beliefs and self-concept (Hughes & Cavell 1999; Madon et al. 2001). Teacher attitudes contribute to the class norms and the references by which students judge each other (Hughes, Cavell & Willson 2001). On the one hand, many of John's teachers did not like him or his behaviour, influencing his social status and likability among his peers. Simply, the way teachers treated John influenced the peer group, who also perceived and treated him in accordance with expectations that he was a 'bully' and 'trouble'. This in turn appeared to influence and reinforce his persistent bullying behaviour.

On the other hand, Brooke and Abbie described teachers who actively supported the bully or ignored/removed the victim. Such actions provide the bully with status and power among the school community and disempower the victim, impacting on the self-concepts of both bully and victims.

Self-concept of those who bully

In order to understand why some students persistently bully and others do not it is helpful to consider both internal and external factors, of which one internal factor is the Self. The Self is a point of reference mediating social experiences and organizing an individual's behaviour towards others. The Self is not a unitary construct, rather the 'personal' self (or personal identity) and the 'social' self form two primary elements. The social self is underpinned by the need to belong and is derived from interpersonal relationships and membership of larger groups such as those of ethnicity and culture (Baumeister & Leary 1995). Many factors, such as genetics, contribute to the development of an individual's self-concept, however none is more influential than interactions with others. Reference groups and significant others act as a mirror and, according to Cooley's looking-glass theory (1998), individuals view themselves as a reflection of how others perceive them (Gecas & Schwalbe 1983). Attributions, particularly those of significant others, play a powerful role when developing one's self-concept. Individuals make self-evaluations based on the effect of their actions, whether good or bad, the role that they play, social and contextual demands, as well as the opinions and behaviours of others around them (Raven & Rubin 1976). A reciprocal relationship also exists between the way an individual behaves and others' perceptions and actions (Bandura 1973).

In this book, self-concept was explored with the young participants by inviting them to discuss their interests, proudest moments, biggest regrets and how they and others perceive them. An individual's proudest moments contribute towards their self-image as they are based on self/other comparisons (Pajares & Schunk 2001). Articulating proudest moments demonstrates an ability to identify areas of success (Schunk, Pintrich & Meece 2008). For John, peer rejection resulted in limited and negative self/other comparisons. It was quite concerning that he found it difficult to recall times when he felt proud and had never experienced '*that bursting of pride*'.

Most participants demonstrated positive self-concepts, describing themselves favourably. However, John – and to a lesser degree, Rebecca – used solely negative adjectives when asked to describe how they thought their parents and teachers perceived them; for example '*very disruptive in class …. the trouble kid … always getting into trouble*'. Furthermore, for Rebecca and John, an already negative self-concept was compounded by the rejection they experienced from their respective peer groups. Often, it is possible for a child to have a negative self-concept at school but a more positive one at home where parents view their child more positively. However, in John's case his mother was a teacher at his school and shared the school community's negative perceptions of him. Sharing a positive relationship with his father may have helped to counteract John's negative self-concept, but unfortunately father and son were not close and even today John is unsure how his father perceives him.

In contrast to Rebecca and John, other participants described family, teachers or peers who viewed them positively, establishing and confirming their positive self-view and affecting their behaviour. For Samantha, close relationships with parents, teachers and peers enabled her to feel confident. By her own account, this was one reason why she ceased bullying others.

Self-verification and reputation enhancement

According to the theory of reciprocal determinism, there is continuous interaction between an individual's cognitions, their environment and the way they behave (Bandura 1973). Accordingly, interactions and relationships with others play a crucial role in the formation of one's behaviour and self-concept. Once an individual's self-concept is formed, they will actively seek information to confirm this and will reject contradictory evidence, thus gaining a sense of equilibrium (North & Swann 2009). Those who develop a negative self-concept will strive to verify this by acting in a way that further alienates them from their peers and others (De La Ronde & Swann 1996). Due to others' perceptions, John developed a negative self-concept which he actively sought to verify by acting in a way that confirmed their views and fulfilled their expectations: the cycle continued (North & Swann 2009). Despite John's strong desire for acceptance and belonging, his behaviour further alienated him from his peers. Overriding the need to belong was the need for status and self-verification.

Self-image, particularly among his peers, became very important to John. This is not unusual, as pre-adolescent males typically choose status and identity over friendship (La Fontana & Cillessen 2009). In order to be seen as 'cool' and 'funny' John behaved as the class clown, thus achieving the status and identity he was looking for. Concurrently, John was developing a public reputation of being a 'bully' and 'trouble'. Peers further enhanced his reputation by spreading the word that he was powerful, setting up a cycle that was presumably difficult to break. Although this reputation may appear negative, it fulfilled John's social goals. It is important to avoid stereotyping or judging John, but rather use his insights to develop proactive relational approaches to support him and others in building the connection and belonging they desire.

Chapter summary

Chapter 10 connected multiple perspectives with well-evidenced literature to highlight the significance of relationships in the lives of young people. While individuals and contexts cannot be directly compared, we have investigated the relational perspectives of a desister, bully and persistent bully to provide a snapshot that informs our understanding of their lived experiences.

Relationships offer a practice ground upon which to learn and rehearse social skills while providing a sense of belonging, thus significantly influencing an individual's identity. For some participants, relationships served as buffers and support, while for others they led to victimization and bullying. Although many of these young people shared positive relationships in one or more domains of their lives (e.g. family, teachers or peers), John consistently reported difficulties in his relationships with adults (parents and teachers) and peers. Leah, Brooke, Abbie, Rebecca and John's difficult peer relationships led to their rejection, victimization, loneliness and bullying, disrupting their search for acceptance and belonging. John subsequently went to extremes to fulfil this fundamental need whereas Leah, Brooke and Abbie chose not to disclose bullying for fear of further rejection and victimization. In essence, neither of these responses contributes to healthy relationship formation with potential influences on wellbeing and academic achievement. In seeking to address persistent bullying we need to be mindful that 'wellbeing is something we all aim for, underpinned by positive notions, yet is unique to each of us and provides us with a sense of who we are which needs to be respected' (Price & McCallum 2016, p. 6).

Having discussed the important role that relationships can play in reinforcing persistent bullying, Chapter 11 will share the turning points and chain reactions that arguably alter an individual's life course.

References

Baldry, A.C. & Farrington, D.P. (1999) Types of bullying among Italian school children. *Journal of Adolescence*, 22(3), pp. 423–426.

Baldry, A.C. & Farrington, D.P. (2000) Bullies and delinquents: Personal characteristics and parenting styles. *Journal of Community and Applied Social Psychology*, 10(1), pp. 17–31.

Bandura, A. (1973) *Aggression: A social learning analysis*. Englewood Cliffs, NJ: Prentice Hall.

Baumeister, R.F. & Leary, M.R. (1995) The need to belong: Desire for interpersonal attachments as a fundamental human motivation. *Psychological Bulletin*, 117(3), pp. 497–529.

Bollmer, J.M., Milich, R., Harris, M.J. & Maras, M.A. (2005) A friend in need: The role of friendship quality as a protective factor in peer victimization and bullying. *Journal of Interpersonal Violence*, 20(6), pp. 701–712.

Bowers, L., Smith, P.K. & Binney, V. (1994) Perceived family relationships of bullies, victims and bully/victims in middle childhood. *Journal of Social and Personal Relationships*, 11(2), pp. 215–232.

Burns, S., Maycock, B., Cross, D. & Brown, G. (2008) The power of peers: Why some students bully others to conform. *Qualitative Health Research*, 18(12), pp. 1704–1716.

Carroll, A., Hattie, J., Durkin, K. & Houghton, S. (2001) Goal-setting and reputation enhancement: Behavioural choices among delinquent, at-risk and not at-risk adolescents. *Legal and Criminological Psychology*, 6(2), pp. 165–184.

Cenkseven Onder, F. & Yurtal, F. (2008) An investigation of the family characteristics of bullies, victims, and positively behaving adolescents. *Educational Sciences: Theory and Practice*, 8(3), pp. 821–832.

Chan, L. (2003) Variable effects of children's aggression, social withdrawal, and prosocial leadership as functions of teacher beliefs and behaviors. *Child Development*, 74(2), pp. 535–548.

Cohen, D. & Strayer, J. (1996) Empathy in conduct-disordered and comparison youth. *Developmental Psychology*, 32(6), pp. 988–998.

Cooley, C.H. (1998) *On self and social organization*. Chicago, IL: University Of Chicago Press.

Craig, W.M. & Pepler, D.J. (2007) Understanding bullying: From research to practice. *Canadian Psychology*, 48(2), pp. 86–93.

Davis, H.A. (2003) Conceptualizing the role and influence of student–teacher relationships on children's social and cognitive development. *Educational Psychologist*, 38(4), pp. 207–234.

De La Ronde, C. & Swann, W.B. (1996) Caught in the crossfire: Positivity and self-verification strivings among people with low self-esteem. In R.F. Baumeister (ed), *Self-esteem: The puzzle of low self-regard*. New York, NY: Plenum Press, pp. 147–165.

de Wied, M., Branje, S.J.T. & Meeus, W.H.J. (2007) Empathy and conflict resolution in friendship relations among adolescents. *Aggressive Behavior*, 33(1), pp. 48–55.

Dodge, K.A., Lansford, J.E., Burks, V.S., Bates, J.E., Pettit, G.S., Fontaine, R. & Price, J.M. (2003) Peer rejection and social information-processing factors in the development of aggressive behavior problems in children. *Child Development*, 74(2), pp. 374–393.

Ellis, B.J., Del Giudice, M., Dishion, T.J., Figueredo, A.J., Gray, P., Griskevicius, V., Hawley, P.H., Jacobs, W.J., James, J. & Volk, A.A. (2012) The evolutionary basis of risky adolescent behavior: Implications for science, policy, and practice. *Developmental Psychology*, 48(3), pp. 598–623.

Emler, N. (1984) Differential involvement in delinquency: Toward an interpretation in terms of reputation management. In B.A. Maher & W.B. Maher (eds), *Progress in experimental personality research, vol. 13*. New York, NY: Academic Press, pp. 173–237.

Eslea, M., Menesini, E., Morita, Y., O'Moore, M., Mora-Mercha, J.A., Pereira, B. & Smith, P.K. (2004) Friendship and loneliness among bullies and victims: Data from seven countries. *Aggressive Behavior*, 30(1), pp. 71–83.

Feshbach, N.D. (1975) Empathy in children: Some theoretical and empirical considerations. *The Counseling Psychologist*, 5(2), pp. 25–30.

Flaspohler, P.D., Elfstrom, J.L., Vanderzee, K.L., Sink, H.E. & Birchmeier, Z. (2009) Stand by me: The effect of peer and teacher support in mitigating the impact of bullying on quality of life. *Psychology in the Schools*, 46(7), pp. 636–649.

Gecas, V. & Schwalbe, M.L. (1983) Beyond the looking-glass self: Social structure and efficacy-based self-esteem. *Social Psychology Quarterly*, 46(2), pp. 77–88.

Gini, G. (2006) Social cognition and moral cognition in bullying: What's wrong? *Aggressive Behavior*, 32(6), pp. 528–539.

Green, D.M., Oswald, M. & Spears, B. (2007) Teachers' (mis)understandings of resilience. *International Education Journal*, 8(2), pp. 133–144.

Huesmann, L.R. (1988) An information processing model for the development of aggression. *Aggressive Behavior*, 14(1), pp. 13–24.

Hughes, J.N. & Cavell, T.A. (1999) Influence of the teacher-student relationship in childhood conduct problems: A prospective study. *Journal of Clinical Child Psychology*, 28(2), pp. 173–184.

Hughes, J.N., Cavell, T.A. & Willson, V. (2001) Further support for the developmental significance of the quality of the teacher–student relationship. *Journal of School Psychology*, 39(4), pp. 289–301.

Hymel, S., Wagner, E. & Butler, L.J. (1990) Reputational bias: View from the peer group. In S.R. Asher & J.D. Coie (eds) *Peer rejection in childhood*. Cambridge: Press Syndicate of the University of Cambridge, pp. 156–186.

Juvonen, J., Graham, S. & Schuster, M.A. (2003) Bullying among young adolescents: The strong, the weak, and the troubled. *Pediatrics*, 112(6), pp. 1231–1237.

Konishi, C., Hymel, S., Zumbo, B.D. & Li, Z. (2010) Do school bullying and student–teacher relationships matter for academic achievement?: A multi-level analysis. *Canadian Journal of School Psychology*, 25(1), pp. 19–39.

Kowalski, R.M., Giumetti, G.W., Schroeder, A.N. & Lattanner, M.R. (2014) Bullying in the digital age: A critical review and meta-analysis of cyberbullying research among youth. *Psychological Bulletin*, 140(4). Available from http://dx.doi.org/10.1037/a0035618, accessed 23 January 2014.

La Fontana, K.M. & Cillessen, A.H.N. (2009) Children's perceptions of popular and unpopular peers: A multimethod assessment. *Developmental Psychology*, 38(5), pp. 635–647.

Ladd, G.W. (1999) Peer relationships and social competence during early and middle childhood. *Annual Review of Psychology*, 50(1), pp. 333–359.

Larrance, D.T. & Twentyman, C.T. (1983) Maternal attributions and child abuse. *Journal of Abnormal Psychology*, 92(4), pp. 449–457.

Loeber, R. & Dishion, T.J. (1984) Boys who fight at home and school: Family conditions influencing cross-setting consistency. *Journal of Consulting and Clinical Psychology*, 52(5), pp. 759–768.

Madon, S., Smith, A., Jussim, L., Russell, D.W., Eccles, J., Palumbo, P. & Walkiewicz, M. (2001) Am I as you see me or do you see me as I am? Self-fulfilling prophecies and self-verification. *Personality and Social Psychology Bulletin*, 27(9), pp. 1214–1224.

Maslow, A. (1954) *Motivation and personality*. New York, NY: Harper.

McCallum, F. & Price, D. (2010) Well teachers, well students. *Journal of Student Wellbeing*, 4(1), pp. 19–34.

Murray-Harvey, R. & Slee, P.T. (2010) School and home relationships and their impact on school bullying. *School Psychology International*, 31(3), pp. 271–295.

Nesdale, D. & Pickering, K. (2006) Teachers' reactions to children's aggression. *Social Development*, 15(1), pp. 109–127.

Nickerson, A.B., Mele, D. & Princiotta, D. (2008) Attachment and empathy as predictors of roles as defenders or outsiders in bullying interactions. *Journal of School Psychology*, 46(6), pp. 687–703.

Noble, T., McGrath, H., Wyatt, T., Carbines, R. & Robb, L. (2008) *Scoping study into approaches to student well-being: Literature review (Report to the Department of Education, Employment and Workplace Relations)*. Sydney, NSW: Australian Catholic University & Erebus International.

Noddings, N. (1988) An ethic of caring and its implications for instructional arrangements. *American Journal of Education*, 96(2), pp. 215–230.

North, R.J. & Swann, W.B. (2009) Self-verification 360°: Illuminating the light and dark sides. *Self and Identity*, 8(2–3), pp. 131–146.

Olweus, D. (1991) Victimization among school children. In R. Baenninger (ed), *Targets of violence and aggression*. Philadelphia, PA: Temple University, pp. 45–102.

Orpinas, P. & Horne, A.M. (2006) *Bullying prevention: Creating a positive school climate and developing social competence*. Washington, DC: American Psychological Association.

Österman, K.F. (2000) Students' need for belonging in the school community. *Review of Educational Research*, 70(3), pp. 323–367.

Pajares, F. & Schunk, D.H. (2001) Self-beliefs and school success: Self-efficacy, self-concept, and school achievement. In R. Riding & S. Rayner (eds), *Perception*. London: Ablex, pp. 239–266.

Pepler, D.J. (2006) Bullying interventions: A binocular perspective. *Canadian Journal of Child Adolescent Psychiatry*, 15(1), pp. 16–20.

Pepler, D.J., Jiang, D., Craig, W.M. & Connolly, J. (2008) Developmental trajectories of bullying and associated factors. *Child Development*, 79(2), pp. 325–338.

Premack, D. & Woodruff, G. (1978) Does the chimpanzee have a theory of mind? *Behavioural and Brain Sciences*, 1(4), pp. 515–526.

Price, D. & McCallum, F. (2016) Wellbeing in education. In F. McCallum & D. Price (eds), *Nurturing wellbeing development in education: From little things big things grow*. London: Routledge, pp. 1–21.

Raven, B.H. & Rubin, J.Z. (1976) *Social psychology: People in groups*. Oxford: John Wiley & Sons.

Rigby, K. (1994) Psychosocial functioning in families of Australian adolescent schoolchildren involved in bully/victim problems. *Journal of Family Therapy*, 16(2), pp. 173–187.

Rosenthal, R. & Jacobson, L. (1968) Pygmalion in the classroom. *The Urban Review*, 3(1), pp. 16–20.

Schneider, B.H., Atkinson, L. & Tardif, C. (2001) Child–parent attachment and children's peer relations: A quantitative review. *Developmental Psychology*, 37(1), pp. 86–100.

Schunk, D.H., Pintrich, P.R. & Meece, J.L. (2008) *Motivation in education: Theory, research and applications*. Upper Saddle River, NJ: Pearson Prentice Hall.

Smith, P.K., Bowers, L., Binney, V. & Cowie, H. (1993) Relationships of children involved in bully/victim problems at school. In S. Duck (ed), *Learning about relationship processes*. London: SAGE, pp. 184–212.

Stevens, V., De Bourdeaudhuij, I. & Van Oost, P. (2002) Relationship of the family environment to children's involvement in bully/victim problems at school. *Journal of Youth and Adolescence*, 31(6), pp. 419–428.

Sutton, J., Smith, P.K. & Sweetham, J. (1999) Bullying and 'theory of mind': A critique of the 'social skills deficit' view of anti-social behaviour. *Social Development*, 8(1), pp. 117–127.

Szewczyk-Sokolowski, M., Bost, K.K. & Wainwright, A.B. (2005) Attachment, temperament, and preschool children's peer acceptance. *Social Development*, 14(3), pp. 379–397.

Thompson, R.A. & Raikes, H.A. (2003) Toward the next quarter-century: Conceptual and methodological challenges for attachment theory. *Development and Psychopathology*, 15(3), pp. 691–718.

Troy, M. & Sroufe, L.A. (1987) Victimization among preschoolers: Role of attachment relationship history. *Journal of the American Academy of Child & Adolescent Psychiatry*, 26(2), pp. 166–172.

Unnever, J.D. & Cornell, D.G. (2004) Middle school victims of bullying: Who reports being bullied? *Aggressive Behavior*, 30(5), pp. 373–388.

Updegraff, K.A., Madden-Derdich, D.A., Estrada, A., Sales, L.J. & Leonard, S.A. (2002) Young adolescents' experiences with parents and friends: Exploring the connections. *Family Relations*, 51, pp. 72–80.

Walden, L.M. & Beran, T.N. (2010) Attachment quality and bullying behavior in school-aged youth. *Canadian Journal of School Psychology*, 25(1), pp. 5–18.

Wentzel, K.R. (1997) Student motivation in middle school: The role of perceived pedagogical caring. *Journal of Educational Psychology*, 89(3), pp. 411–419.

11
TURNING POINTS AND CHAIN REACTIONS

Exploring the life trajectories of those who bully and those who are targeted by bullying behaviour offers new insights in understanding and addressing the phenomenon of persistent bullying. In relation to those who bully, are victimized or desist, distinct trajectories have been identified. For victims, these trajectories include:

- non–victims: low levels of victimization
- desisters: high levels of victimization which decrease over time
- late onset: victimization increases over time
- stable victims: high levels of victimization over time

(Goldbaum, Craig, Pepler &
Connolly 2003)

As previously noted, similar trajectories were found among those who bully (Pepler et al. 2008):

- starts low and increases
- starts moderate and desists
- starts moderate and remains moderate (persistent)
- starts high and remains high (persistent)

Interestingly, of the 871 children involved in Pepler et al.'s (2008) study, 41.6 per cent reported almost never bullying; 35.1 per cent reported bullying at consistently moderate levels; 9.9 per cent reported consistently high levels of bullying; and 13.4 per cent reported moderate levels in adolescence but had desisted to almost no bullying at the end of high school. What are the turning points that influence these trajectories? While turning points have been considered in relation to the concept of resilience (Johnson & Howard 2007), various elements underpinning this theory can be applied to bullying. Therefore, this chapter aims to highlight the turning points and chain reactions in the lives of the young people who have been the focus of this book.

What are turning points?

Biases in social information-processing and/or coping strategies together with peer relationship difficulties place a student at the most risk of bullying or being bullied (Dodge et al. 2003; Marini et al. 2006). However, a unitary risk factor may not necessarily determine whether a student will bully or be bullied. When there is a series of risk factors the chance of engaging in bullying or being bullied increases (Garmezy 1993). Rutter (1996) proposed that risk factors interact, creating negative chain reactions which shape a person's trajectory. Turning points refer to events that occur in an individual's life that either positively or negatively alter their life trajectory. Three categories of turning points are suggested: those that either shut down or open up opportunities (such as dropping out of school at a young age); those that involve a lasting change in one's environment (such as the death of a significant other); and those that have a lasting effect on a person's self-concept (such as peer rejection) (Rutter 1996). These turning points involve 'marked environmental or organismic discontinuity' (Rutter 1996, p. 15) and are persistent enough to effect change over time, thus impacting on an individual's development. For example, early menarche in females can form a turning point that may lead to norm-breaking behaviours later in life (Caspi & Moffitt 1991). Chain reactions refer to a series of turning points that together change an individual's trajectory (Rutter 1996).

Positive turning points can change a person's life course favourably (Gilligan 2009). However, negative experiences commonly occur in clusters and are interconnected in some way (Rutter 1999) where:

> The extent of environmental risk exposure is determined in part by societal circumstances but above all it is influenced by how people themselves behave. By their actions, people do much to shape and select their experiences. In this way, vicious circles build up.
>
> (p. 129)

Vicious circles were particularly evident in Brooke and John's cases. Therefore it is important to consider the interaction among turning points as it shifts the focus from the individual to the roles played by the environment and circumstances.

Gilligan (2000) describes turning points: 'like a yacht on a journey, the young person's development may be blown off course by unfavourable incidents or winds, and back on course if conditions turn more favourable' (p. 38). This approach challenges our thinking by providing a means of considering life events and circumstances in a child's life as factors that may positively or negatively influence their behaviour, providing a platform to focus on broader aspects of the child's life as opposed to concentrating solely on the individual, their behaviour and their family. We begin by looking at the potential turning points in the life of Leah, a self-identified victim.

Potential turning points in the life of Leah (victim)

Negative turning points and chain reactions can be identified in Leah's life. While living in Queensland as a baby, her father passed away. Losing a parent may place a child at risk of psychosocial maladaptation (Garmezy & Rutter 1983). A year before the interview, Leah and her family moved to South Australia to make a fresh start. For her, this transition was extremely difficult and was further compounded by peer rejection and exclusion. In Leah's case, personal loss, her recent family move, as well as peer rejection potentially contributed to her being the victim of ongoing bullying. At the time of our conversation, Leah had not fostered any positive chain reactions and therefore could be at risk of further victimization and poor psychosocial development (Rutter 1996).

Leah experienced rejection from the majority of her peer group. She found making and maintaining friendships difficult and lacked the practice ground to learn and rehearse the necessary social skills to achieve this. Although she viewed exclusion as a motive to make new friends, it negatively affected her school life. Unfortunately Leah also experienced exclusion by those outside of school which further contributed to her unhappiness and low sense of belonging. Schooling aims to provide a happy environment which is associated with energy, high self-esteem, emotional stability, positive social relationships and reduced fear, hostility, anxiety and anger (Michalos 2008). Leah would need to acquire a range of social skills necessary to gain and maintain friends and contribute to her happiness; however this alone will not address the problem. All students in her class need to participate in social skills training in order to ensure that Leah is not singled out as being different from her peers and the only person requiring development. Furthermore, a cohesive classroom climate where everyone is accepted for who they are is also needed. This will enable Leah, along with her peers, to gain the necessary social skills while also providing a safe, inclusive environment in which to practise them.

As mentioned previously, developing a positive relationship with teachers can act as a buffer against future victimization. However, Leah became attached to her teacher and decided to spend time interacting with her during recess and lunch. While this potentially strengthened the student–teacher relationship, it further alienated her from her peers, thus appearing to increase her chances of being bullied. Such negative chain reactions require overturning, with teachers monitoring and facilitating the development of positive student–teacher and peer-to-peer relationships. Promoting a classroom climate where students accept and respect individual differences contributes to the wellbeing of all (Price & McCallum 2016b). By facilitating such a classroom climate, a team spirit can be fostered among students, which will encourage them to protect and support each other.

Students such as Leah would benefit from a whole-school approach to promoting a positive, inclusive school ecology (Price & McCallum 2016b). Recognition that we are all unique – yet more alike than we are different – could be fostered among school leaders, teachers, students, parents and the larger community. In this way difference is celebrated, rather than contributing to rejection. Proactive whole-school initiatives to prevent persistent bullying operate at the levels of the school community, the classroom and the individual (Price & McCallum 2016a).

Potential turning points in the life of Brooke (a persistent victim)

For Brooke, the first chain reaction occurred when she was in Year 4. Like most children, she started school full of excitement; however, in Year 4 her parents separated as a result of her father's disclosure of homosexuality. This occurred at a time when homosexuality was rarely discussed in a healthy manner, placing Brooke's family at the centre of rumours and gossip. Around this time, her brother was involved in a near-fatal accident and she became his primary carer. These two life-changing events transformed Brooke from a happy, carefree nine-year-old girl to a young person struggling with complex issues and responsibilities. Consequently, she was perceived as being different from her peers, which led to her being victimized. Once Brooke reached high school, her peers began to understand what it meant for her father to be homosexual and the bullying escalated. To compensate, Brooke began acting promiscuously, which attracted further bullying. These life-changing events were out of Brooke's control, yet they triggered a chain reaction that altered her life course. To disrupt this process, positive chain reactions needed to be fostered. For Brooke, this involved joining her local church where she developed new friendships and gained a sense of belonging and reprieve from persistent bullying.

Potential turning points in the life of Abbie (bully/victim)

For Abbie, bullying started because she was perceived to be different from her peers. Abbie came from a different cultural background and her parents were strict about who she interacted with and where she was able to go. This left her feeling isolated from her peers. Her relationship with her parents was not close and this placed her at further risk of being victimized (Orpinas & Horne 2006; Perren & Hornung 2005; Perry, Hodges & Egan 2001; Stevens, De Bourdeaudhuij & Van Oost 2002). In addition, Abbie didn't have a 'best' friend and although she appeared to have a number of friends, they seemingly lacked the ability, skills or confidence to defend her when she was being bullied, which left her feeling alone and powerless. In Abbie's eyes, something needed to change. She began engaging in risky behaviours as a means of interacting and befriending those perceived as powerful in the peer group. Unfortunately this only led to further bullying. Therefore, to increase her status and power among her peers, Abbie, unlike Leah and Brooke, started bullying those she considered weaker and less powerful than her.

For the cycle of victimization and bullying to stop Abbie needed positive turning points. Abbie eventually confided in her parents and sought their help. Together, they agreed that she should spend her final years in a different school which embraced a 'team-like' inclusive ethos where everyone was accepted and cared for. With this change to a more accepting and supportive school, Abbie was no longer targeted, therefore ceased bullying others.

Potential turning points in the life of Rebecca (a bully)

Turning points and chain reactions are equally important in the lives of those who bully. There were two significant chain reactions in Rebecca's life, the first occurring when her parents divorced. Rebecca found it difficult to cope without her father and was left feeling angry and frustrated. Parental conflict has been identified as a risk factor for engaging in bullying (Baldry & Farrington 2000). The second chain reaction involved Rebecca's difficulties in socializing with peers; she felt excluded and isolated. Lacking a sense of belonging, Rebecca engaged in bullying as she strived to gain acceptance. To buffer these negative experiences, positive chain reactions need to be fostered, but this had not yet occurred at the time of our conversation. Like Leah, Rebecca needs the opportunity to learn and practise prosocial skills alongside and inclusive of her peers.

Potential turning points in the life of John (a persistent bully)

Three negative turning points appeared to shape and reinforce John's bullying behaviour. The first commenced when John started school. While Abbie was perceived as different by her peer group due to her cultural background, John was considered different because of his large stature. As a result he was socially rejected by his peer group, and this continued throughout his school life. John's mother was a teacher who taught at different schools every couple of years. These frequent school moves added a further dimension to John's peer relationship difficulties. Teachers often paired him with other new students in an attempt to help him make friends, however this strategy was unsuccessful.

Without sufficient time in one school and opportunities to learn crucial social skills such as gaining and maintaining friendships, John remained unsuccessful in his peer relationships throughout his school life. This rejection influenced his behaviour, both in and out of the classroom. Having any interaction with his peers, whether negative or positive, was important to John. These interactions often included bullying, which further isolated him from his peers and contributed to his relationship difficulties with his teachers and parents.

The second chain reaction in John's life is closely related to the first. He used his large stature as a means of interacting with peers, allowing them to physically attack him. From John's perspective, this provided him with a form of acceptance and a sense of belonging. As a result, John started bullying, believing this would entertain his peers and increase his acceptance and connectedness.

The third and final chain reaction involves issues of identity, reputation and self-concept. The need to gain any attention from peers and others and to develop an identity underpinned John's bullying behaviour. Consequently, his teachers and peers perceived and treated him as 'trouble'. Even his own parents expected him to do the wrong thing, leading him to consider himself as a 'trouble kid' and a bully. The attitude and behaviour of the school community served to enhance this self-image, something that was important for John as he struggled to belong. A cycle developed whereby he continued to bully and misbehave to fulfil these expectations. As a result, he was increasingly reprimanded, further enhancing his self-concept and reputation among the peer group and school community. Persistent bullying served to maintain his reputation, power and status among his peers and for John, this was an adaptive behaviour (Ellis et al. 2012). The cycle appeared to remain unbroken.

Potential turning points in the life of Samantha (a desister)

While Samantha and her friend engaged in low levels of bullying in pre-school, she stopped bullying in about Year 4, unlike John and Rebecca. Although this change in behaviour could be attributed to maturation, positive turning points may also have played a role. The first turning point centred on Samantha's ability to gain and maintain friendships. Unlike John and Rebecca, Samantha started school with a best friend and a wide circle of close friends. When her best friend changed schools in Year 4, Samantha readily established new friendships. Although Samantha later changed schools numer-ous times, she found these transitions easy, unlike John. She joined various sporting activities and her circle of friends expanded. Samantha had the necessary social skills to develop and maintain friendships, providing the environment offered opportunity to practise and refine her skills, but these factors were clearly missing in John's life.

The second turning point in Samantha's life centred on family. Samantha shared a very close relationship with her immediate and extended family, which provided a source of support and guidance when needed. Her parents appeared to adopt an authoritative parenting approach where they discussed behaviour and modelled what was expected. Samantha was never expected to get into trouble, however when she did her parents encouraged her to think about how others may feel. Encouraging Samantha to recognize the impact of her behaviour made her realize 'oh this is how I have made people feel' which in turn encouraged her to stop bullying. This capacity to empathize was lacking in John's case. Together these positive chain reactions led Samantha to stop bullying others. One can only ponder whether simi-lar positive experiences could have altered John's life course.

Chapter summary

These case studies have provided insights into the possible mechanisms and turning points at play in the lives of young people who experience bullying as either victims or perpetrators. In contrasting Samantha's and John's lives, one wonders what John's trajectory would have been like if successful group entry and other social skills had been acquired. Would John's behaviour have differed if the school community, and particularly his teachers and parents, had viewed him more positively, identifying and highlighting his strengths as opposed to his perceived shortcomings? Similarly, had Brooke been provided with support from her family, school and friends, would she have endured relentless bullying? What would her life and future have been like had she not become involved in the church?

Samantha, Abbie, Brooke and John have highlighted the importance of fostering positive turning points in the lives of young people who are bullied or who bully others. By spending time supporting and nurturing protective mechanisms it is possible that we can change young people's lives for the better. Using inclusive approaches, schools, teachers and counsellors need to strive to ensure that students develop a sense of belonging and the necessary social skills. We therefore suggest that a more proactive strategy, which recognizes possible turning points, may reduce the likelihood of persistent bullying occurring. We further explore proactive approaches in Chapter 12: *Educational implications*, to move forward in our endeavour to reduce persistent bullying in schools.

References

Baldry, A.C. & Farrington, D.P. (2000) Bullies and delinquents: Personal characteristics and parenting styles. *Journal of Community and Applied Social Psychology*, 10(1), pp. 17–31.

Caspi, A. & Moffitt, T.E. (1991) Individual differences are accentuated during periods of social change: The sample case of girls at puberty. *Journal of Personality and Social Psychology*, 61(1), pp. 157–168.

Dodge, K.A., Lansford, J.E., Burks, V.S., Bates, J.E., Pettit, G.S., Fontaine, R. & Price, J.M. (2003) Peer rejection and social information-processing factors in the development of aggressive behavior problems in children. *Child Development*, 74(2), pp. 374–393.

Ellis, B.J., Del Giudice, M., Dishion, T.J., Figueredo, A.J., Gray, P., Griskevicius, V., Hawley, P.H., Jacobs, W.J., James, J. & Volk, A.A. (2012) The evolutionary basis of risky adolescent behavior: Implications for science, policy, and practice. *Developmental Psychology*, 48(3), pp. 598–623.

Garmezy, N. (1993) Children in poverty: Resilience despite risk. *Psychiatry*, 56(1), pp. 127–136.

Garmezy, N. & Rutter, M. (eds) (1983) *Stress, coping, and development in children*. New York, NY: McGraw Hill.

Gilligan, R. (2000) Adversity, resilience and young people: The protective value of positive school and spare time experiences. *Children & Society*, 14(1), pp. 37–47.

Gilligan, R. (2009) Positive turning points in the dynamics of change over the life course. In J.A. Mancini & K.A. Roberto (eds), *Pathways of human development: Explorations of change*. Plymouth, UK: Lexington Books, pp. 15–34.

Goldbaum, S., Craig, W.M., Pepler, D. & Connolly, J. (2003) Developmental trajectories of victimization: Identifying risk and protective factors. *Journal of Applied School Psychology*, 19(2), pp. 139–156.

Johnson, B. & Howard, S. (2007). Causal chain effects and turning points in young people's lives: A resilience perspective. *Journal of Student Wellbeing*, 1(2), pp. 1–15.

Marini, Z.A., Dane, A.V., Bosacki, S.L. & YLC-CURA (2006) Direct and indirect bully-victims: Differential psychosocial risk factors associated with adolescents involved in bullying and victimization. *Aggressive Behavior*, 32(6), pp. 551–569.

Michalos, A.C. (2008) Education, happiness and wellbeing. *Social Indicators Research*, 87(3), pp. 347–366.

Orpinas, P. & Horne, A.M. (2006) *Bullying prevention: Creating a positive school climate and developing social competence*. Washington, DC: American Psychological Association.

Pepler, D., Jiang, D., Craig, W., & Connolly, J. (2008) Developmental trajectories of bullying and associated factors. *Child Development*, 79(2), pp. 325–338.

Perren, S. & Hornung, R. (2005) Bullying and delinquency in adolescence: Victims' and perpetrators' family and peer relations. *Swiss Journal of Psychology*, 64(1), pp. 51–64.

Perry, D.G., Hodges, E.V.E. & Egan, S.K. (2001) Determinants of chronic victimization by peers: A review and new model of family influence. In J. Juvonen & S. Graham (eds), *Peer harassment in school: The plight of the vulnerable and victimized*. New York, NY: The Guilford Press, pp. 73–104.

Price, D. & McCallum, F. (2016a) Leading and empowering lifelong wellbeing: Well educators, well learners, well communities. In F. McCallum & D. Price (eds), *Nurturing wellbeing development in education: From little things big things grow*. London: Routledge, pp.133–145.

Price, D. & McCallum, F. (2016b) Wellbeing in education. In F. McCallum & D. Price (eds), *Nurturing wellbeing development in education: From little things big things grow*. London: Routledge, pp. 1–21.

Rutter, M. (1996) Transitions and turning points in developmental psychopathology: As applied to the age span between childhood and mid-adulthood. *International Journal of Behavioral Development*, 19(3), pp. 603–626.

Rutter, M. (1999) Resilience concepts and findings: Implications for family therapy. *Journal of Family Therapy*, 21(2), pp. 119–144.

Stevens, V., De Bourdeaudhuij, I. & Van Oost, P. (2002) Relationship of the family environment to children's involvement in bully/victim problems at school. *Journal of Youth and Adolescence*, 31(6), pp. 419–428.

12

EDUCATIONAL IMPLICATIONS

Multiple Perspectives in Persistent Bullying: Capturing and listening to young people's voices has focused on the lived experiences of victims, bully/victims, a desister, bystanders, a bully and a persistent bully. In essence, it has exposed the significant impact of bullying on young lives. These case studies have also highlighted the complex interplay between belonging, relationships, power, family and environmental factors. For some, the turning points and chain reactions were significant in contributing to positive outcomes, while for others, a spiral of negative chain reactions occurred, resulting in persistent bullying or victimization. In this final chapter, we consider educational approaches to addressing this significant phenomenon.

Bullying interventions implemented through schools have not been universally successful (Farrington & Ttofi 2009; Kumpulainen, Räsänen & Henttonen 1999; Pepler et al. 2008; Rigby 2002, 2011; Smith & Shu 2000; Ttofi & Farrington 2011) and some students continue to bully in spite of such interventions. Persistent, unrelenting bullying negatively affects the wellbeing of all stakeholders (Green 2015).

Given the educational priority to provide safe and engaging school environments conducive to optimum learning and wellbeing, persistent bullies compromise this environment and we suggest that this needs urgent action. The students participating in Green's (2015) study described how classroom climate can become unsafe and is constantly disrupted. Parent perspectives support such notions, with one parent describing how persistent bullies are '*disruptive; they don't care whether others learn or not*'. Teachers also shared how '*continuous disciplinary issues*' detract from teaching and learning with one experienced female middle-years teacher stating how persistent bullies '*take away valuable teaching time*'. These teachers reported feeling stressed, frustrated and lacking the self-efficacy needed to manage persistent bullies (Green 2015). This, coupled with an increase in time spent managing the learning environment, left teachers feeling drained. Referring to students considered persistent troublemakers, school counsellors explained that teachers '*get sick of him/her*', a message that is often transmitted to peers and to bullies themselves. These teachers describe difficult and often confrontational relationships with those who persistently bully. Of real concern is evidence suggesting that there is a widespread belief among students that persistent bullying cannot be stopped, as reported by students across Reception to Year 9 in a large qualitative study (Green 2015), and also shared by the bystanders presented in this book. Therefore, to improve the wellbeing of all concerned and enhance learning in a safe school environment, proactive positive approaches that are based on nuanced understandings of persistent bullies need to be developed.

Part V concludes by discussing educational implications of persistent bullying and victimization, posing questions and suggesting areas for future exploration to inform educational practice, policy and research.

Implications for policy and practice

In recent years, policies and approaches to reduce the prevalence of bullying have been introduced through multiple educational and government initiatives. In Australia, these initiatives include peer mentoring, individual behaviour plans, bullying audits, whole-school frameworks such as *KidsMatter* (Commonwealth of Australia 2008) and *MindMatters* (Australian Government Department of Health 2014), as well as zero tolerance school policies. However, despite these initiatives a proportion of students continue to persistently bully. Teachers and counsellors report feeling underequipped when working with persistent bullies, highlighting a need for further support, professional development and training for pre-service teachers (Green 2015).

While early proactive intervention is necessary, we emphasize that bullies do not form one homogenous group, therefore packaged interventions may not address all of those who persistently bully. A three-tiered approach to positive behaviour is needed. The first tier includes a whole-school intervention that targets the entire school community; a second tier engages those students who do not respond to the first tier and thus require a more targeted intervention; and a third tier which is designed for the small number of students who have not responded to the other two tiers and thus need an intensive approach (Horner, Todd, Lewis-Palmer, Irvin, Sugai & Boland 2004). This approach recognizes that while classroom interventions may be successful with the majority of students, those identified as being in a high risk category are best served using individualized strategies. Given that persistent bullies form part of the latter category, individualized programmes may hold the key to addressing persistent bullying as 'one size does not fit all'. To achieve this, further funding and resourcing may include supporting a team of professionals who work with schools, families and individual students to reduce persistent bullying. In addition to increased external professional support, it is vital to increase the professional expertise of internal school personnel: for example, by employing trained counsellors or psychologists. Schools around the world increasingly appoint experts with some counselling, social work and/or psychology qualifications in order to help support students and staff. However, in some regions, such specialization is preferred but not required. For example, most South Australian school counsellors are qualified teachers who may or may not have any counselling qualifications (Howard 2014; Kay 2014, personal communications). This is a system-level issue which impacts on a school's ability to fund the appointment of personnel who can lead proactive educational initiatives across whole-school communities. Given the escalating concern with persistent bullying, mandatory levels of training for counsellors are needed. In addition, pre-service teachers need compulsory training in bullying, relationships and inclusive education (Price 2016).

While individual educational initiatives may provide positive outcomes, whole-school and national approaches are also considered important. In Australia, the implementation of initiatives such as the *National Safe Schools Framework* in 2004 mandated schools to commit to and implement anti-bullying policies. To enhance the implementation of this framework, the Australian Government provided funding to some schools. However, in research conducted four years after this mandate, Cross et al. (2011) found that, although the majority of schools in their study had developed anti-bullying policies, only 25 per cent of staff reported being aware of the policy content. Schools that received funding and implemented policies recorded positive outcomes, while personnel in schools that did not receive funding reported being time and resource poor which affected the overall success of this initiative. Furthermore, while online digital resources were developed to support the *National Safe Schools Framework*, these may have been under-utilized in addressing issues such as persistent bullying. For example, an evaluation of one such resource, the *Safe Schools Hub* (SSH), found that while the resource is valuable, it was not fully utilized due to low visibility and lack of stakeholder awareness (Taddeo et al. 2015).

The success of anti-bullying policies and interventions relies on how they are implemented (Rigby 2010; Salmivalli, Kaukiainen & Voeten 2005). Successful implementation varies from school to school, making each context unique. Furthermore, school personnel also contribute at different levels and take on varying roles (Ball, Maguire & Braun 2012; Johnson & Sullivan 2014). Implementing policies and interventions that are collegially constructed, contextual and accepted by school personnel and stakeholders is therefore crucial. Schools need to ensure that staff are adequately trained and have the time and necessary leadership support to implement and monitor the intervention (Cross et al. 2011; Orpinas & Horne 2006; Slee et al. 2009). It has been increasingly suggested that the school leadership play a pivotal role in empowering all stakeholders as agents, through their ability to initiate, sustain and advance wellbeing initiatives at both individual and collective levels (Price & McCallum 2016). However, school personnel, students and parents often do not fully understand the interventions being employed (Rigby 2010); therefore it is a fundamental requirement to align initiatives with the expertise and understandings of the stakeholders involved. In addition, the involvement of *all* stakeholders in the community is important in the effective implementation of interventions and frameworks (Slee et al. 2009). School communities are more likely to embrace interventions which align with established procedures that mirror the school's philosophy (Rigby 2010). Therefore it is vital to re-visit school philosophy and consider how it aligns to the endeavour of building positive relationships and a sense of belonging for all members of the school community. Effective implementation determines the success or failure of interventions, therefore considerable time and energy needs to be invested in the early stages.

While Cross et al. (2011) found that many Australian schools had not fully implemented their anti-bullying policies, the schools and stakeholders who contributed to this book demonstrated an understanding of bullying that aligned closely to that of researchers. They were also able to understand the more subtle forms of bullying, suggesting that these schools were positively educating their community. To advance these positive developments, we suggest that anti-bullying education needs to include a focus on those who persistently bully so that stakeholders understand how some behaviours, policies and/or school practices may actually motivate and reinforce bullying, rather than reduce or eliminate it. When members of the school community are able to recognize and take responsibility for actions and policies which may inadvertently reinforce this relentless behaviour, they are one step closer to positive change.

In terms of individualized approaches to those who bully, psychological interventions may be appropriate if supported by family and – crucially – the perpetrator. For example, John's life experiences promoted a poor self-view which seemingly contributed to his persistent bullying. For individuals like John, approaches that address such internal thought processes, for example, cognitive behaviour therapy (CBT), may be appropriate. CBT involves helping individuals to recognize behaviours and thoughts that are unhelpful and to learn or relearn those that are helpful. Simply put, CBT helps individuals alter thought patterns and behaviour (Blenkiron 2013). CBT interventions are typically short, ranging from five to twenty sessions and, in the case of persistent bullies, may need to be conducted in conjunction with social skills training. It is important to address self-verification of negative self-concepts and this may be achieved by accepting and acknowledging the individual's feelings and then providing positive feedback that challenges their negative self-view (North & Swann 2009). Ideally, this is where a professional team, including a qualified school counsellor or psychologist, can work with the student, their family and teachers.

Furthermore, to be successful, schools need to reduce – if not remove – the use of labels to describe students, as labels prevent nuanced understandings of behaviour (Shaughnessy 2012). In writing this book we were challenged by using labels, however the intention was to give voice to these multiple perspectives for a greater understanding, and to challenge stereotypical stigmas. Labels, self-fulfilling prophecies, self-verification and reputation management seemingly played a significant role in John's persistent bullying. Labels often promote stereotypes, influencing the way a student is perceived and treated, which in turn shapes behaviour. Many schools have refrained from using labels and embraced an inclusive ethos, yet, in the case of persistent bullies, this does not appear to have been successful. Many adults clearly hold negative views of persistent bullies with little or no acknowledgement of their individuality (Green 2015), something that possibly contributed to and reinforced their persistent behaviour. Further education is warranted, involving all stakeholders including parents and caregivers, which focuses on developing understandings of the lived experiences of those who persistently bully. This book is a further step in advancing our understanding of the persistent bully's keen desire to belong, to be recognized and to be accepted.

Explicit in John's narrative was the role of identity and reputation enhancement. Identification of those students who have power and those who are rejected may form an important element of the puzzle. In order to address persistent bullying, perpetrators should be scaffolded to undertake leadership and advocacy roles in society in relation to anti-bullying, thus providing healthy opportunities for them to meet social goals, such as status and identity. Accessing their voice and knowledge on best practice serves two purposes: gaining important insights into their behaviour; and developing a more positive reputation among stakeholders. In his narrative, John expressed the need for schools to introduce early education aimed at helping persistent bullies build a positive self-identity. Without such proactive approaches, persistent bullies will continue to be marginalized from their peers and from educational opportunities. Adverse negative causal and external factors within educational contexts, including school processes, achievement-related experiences, and social interactions, will continue to influence and damage wellbeing and further advance educational marginalization (Best 2016; Faubert 2012; Riordan 2006).

Throughout these chapters we have highlighted the importance of relationships. The need to belong influences how individuals view themselves. A lack of social skills, particularly empathy, was highlighted as possibly contributing to persistent bullying. Given the lack of social skills and relationship difficulties that have emerged in some of the narratives, the need to embed inter- and intra-personal skills training in the curriculum is suggested. In the Australian context, this can be aligned with the social and personal capabilities embedded across the Australian Curriculum. Educators are challenged by the pressures of a crowded curriculum and accountability for student achievement outcomes; often these compromise the time and priority placed on personal development. However, we contend that investing in nurturing students' wellbeing and social/emotional capabilities will not only yield improvements in learning outcomes, but will also help to address the problem of bullying in schools.

To further address persistent bullying, multi-media, computer-based training offers a modern, familiar and engaging means of teaching social skills and reducing school violence. Such training has been found to successfully address social skills, including conflict resolution, as well as attributional, behavioural and affective responses, making it an ideal means of reducing persistent bullying (Bosworth, Espelage, DuBay, Daytner & Karageorge 2000; Hobbs & Yan 2008). This approach may be particularly advantageous for persistent bullies as the training takes place in the absence of an audience, thereby minimizing opportunities to enhance a non-conforming reputation. It is important to personalize programmes to ensure that individual students acquire the skills they personally need to be socially competent, while being respectful of their individuality and lived experiences. Such initiatives would also require professional development to increase teachers' understandings of the programme and enable them to offer appropriate support.

Minimizing or trivializing behaviour has been noted in those who bully (Bandura et al. 1996; Hymel, Rocke-Henderson & Bonanno 2005; Menesini et al. 2003). Bullies often use descriptors such as 'just' and 'only' to describe their behaviour (Green 2015). Encouraging students, particularly persistent bullies, to take responsibility for their actions is crucial. Drawing attention to trivializing language could assist in raising awareness, acknowledging bullying as a serious, negative behaviour and encouraging bystanders and the school community to act.

Many participants in Green's (2015) large study suggested that persistent bullies may also be victims, yet little empathy or understanding for them was evident in participant's responses. Understanding and employing empathy towards individual differences is an underdeveloped area in relation to persistent bullying. In the classroom, lessons promoting understanding and respect for diversity are therefore suggested. Adopting a proactive rather than reactive approach to persistent bullying may be further advanced by curriculum and educational policy that embeds and celebrates diversity of identity from an early age. In saying this, when bullying does occur, explicit support for both the victim and bully initially could assist in breaking the victim-to-bully trajectory evidenced in Abbie and John's narratives.

Highlighting the role of reciprocal determinism, we suggest that, rather than merely trying to 'fix' individuals who persistently bully, educators and policymakers need to take ownership for analysing their school culture and policy and to consider whether this reinforces or minimizes persistent bullying. Such initiatives challenge conventional approaches to addressing bullying, such as formal sanctions and zero tolerance policies, which focus on individuals rather than the broader school ecology. While we agree that bullying should definitely not be tolerated, early intervention and proactive educational initiatives involving all stakeholders is vital. That is, if persistent bullying is evident, it is important to question how the school culture is addressing the relationship, identity, status and belonging needs of transgressors. Also, analysing and addressing the roles that bystanders and others play in such experiences could help to break the cycle of persistent bullying. School communities need to take responsibility for a whole-school commitment that strategically supports and educates all stakeholders in addressing this ongoing problem. Listening to the voices of those at the centre is an essential step towards developing and implementing these initiatives and policies.

Moving forward: Further questions and areas for exploration

A number of questions and areas for exploration have emerged from these discussions. As a persistent bully, John's unique voice provides a platform for further research with others who have persistently engaged in anti-social behaviour. John was evidently capable of displaying empathy when explicitly taught, yet found it difficult to initiate this alone. The online environment provides anonymity, therefore the impact that bullying has on victims is not always obvious (Kowalski et al. 2014). This raises questions about the relationship between empathy and persistent bullying in the online context. In addition, further exploration is needed to understand the role played by bystanders and hybrid bystanders: those who are present, observe or move between online and face-to-face environments (Price et al. 2014).

The need to belong has been identified as underpinning and reinforcing persistent bullying. However, the concept of belonging takes on new dimensions in cyberspace. While the online environment can be isolating for some young people, it can provide an avenue for peer acceptance for others. On the one hand, peer rejection – a risk factor for bullying – may be buffered in an online setting. On the other hand, cyberspace has become a particularly harmful environment for bullying. These tensions have yet to be resolved. Adopting a sociometric approach, the social networks of the peer group could be employed to further explore the relationship between long-term rejection and persistent bullying in both traditional and online settings. We know that those who bully in one context often transfer to the other. Why do some bullies operate in both environments, while others do not?

Sharing the voices of key stakeholders has provided insight into their lived experiences and the factors that may reinforce or mitigate the risks of victimization or persistent bullying. We suggest that such first-hand perspectives that capture youth voice will further advance our understandings of bullying, both online and face-to-face, which will in turn inform policy and practice (Spears & Kofoed 2013). The voices presented in Parts II, III and IV have provided unique insights from those at the coal-face. Having young people working with policymakers will, we believe, be a positive step towards addressing persistent bullying.

Longitudinal data on the implementation and evaluation of social skills interventions would shed light on persistent bullying and the need to belong. Following students from early years through to high school could also provide insight into turning points, protective mechanisms and the effectiveness of interventions employed. Computer-based, multi-media programmes targeting social skills need to be developed and tested to determine their effectiveness on persistent bullies.

The exploration of turning points and chain reactions in the lives of these young people who are victimized or who bully others has provided a unique way of considering this behaviour. Studying the lives of others who persistently bully or are victimized may shed further light on similar turning points, possibly informing us of further risk and protective factors associated with persistent bullying. The identification of these life-changing events provides insight into critical times in the lives of young people and will help to inform practice, policy and interventions.

Final thoughts

Over past decades, research into traditional bullying, and now cyberbullying, has relied primarily on a quantitative paradigm (Jimerson, Swearer & Espelage 2010). Mixed method approaches have also been employed, however these have largely centred on content analysis as opposed to accessing the 'voice' of those involved in bullying. We concur with Spears and Kofoed (2013) that youth voice is needed to further understandings of bullying and cyberbullying.

While quantitative studies have highlighted the need to belong as a motivator for bullying, John's narrative advances these studies by providing a more nuanced understanding of the circumstances that have led to his behaviour. John's lived experiences highlighted the powerful role that others' perceptions and labels play in shaping his behaviour. Using theories of self-verification and reputation enhancement as a lens through which to understand persistent bullying contributes to the existing body of knowledge in this area.

A combination of the following theories sheds a unique light on persistent bullying and warrants further research: self-fulfilling prophecies (Merton 1948), self-verification (North & Swann 2009), reputation management (Emler 1984) and reciprocal determinism (Bandura 1973; 1977).

Through self-fulfilling cycles, self-verification and reputation management, persistent bullies seemingly re-engage in bullying, in spite of interventions and sanctions designed to prevent these aggressive acts. For them, bullying appears to be adaptive, meeting their social goals of belonging, status and identity. To address persistent bullying, we have articulated individual approaches which have clear implications for policy and practice.

We hope that *Multiple Perspectives in Persistent Bullying: Capturing and listening to young people's voices* has stimulated you to think critically about bullying and persistent bullying. We hope that you will look at those who bully in a different light by considering the various turning points and chain reactions in their lives that have influenced them to adopt these behaviours. Effective interventions need to accommodate the individuals and the various interconnecting factors that have an impact on behaviour and, importantly, identify the possible role we all may inadvertently play in shaping the perceptions and behaviours of those who bully. In concluding, the voice of John challenges us to address the phenomenon of persistent bullying:

> I think a lot of it comes down to identity … who the student thinks they are … is a big part of it … which is brought about by the teachers and the school. I think punishments sometimes are a bit of an identity … as well I remember going to detention all the time and seeing the same kids and we would talk in class … it was sort of a group you know 'the detention kids' … 'oh what did you do?' … we didn't really care and if you got punished it was just because I'm bad … that's who I am … you can brush it off pretty easily I think and it helps to create who you are as well.

References

Australian Government Department of Health (2014) *MindMatters*. Available from www.mindmatters.edu.au/, accessed 23 January 2016.

Ball, S.J., Maguire, M. & Braun, A. (2012) *How schools do policy: Policy enactments in secondary schools*. London: Routledge.

Bandura, A. (1973) *Aggression: A social learning analysis*. Englewood Cliffs, NJ: Prentice Hall.

Bandura, A. (1977) *Social learning theory*. Englewood Cliffs, NJ: Prentice Hall.

Bandura, A., Barbaranelli, C., Caprara, G.V. & Pastorelli, C. (1996) Mechanisms of moral disengagement in the exercise of moral agency. *Journal of Personality and Social Psychology*, 71(2), pp. 364–374.

Best, M. (2016) Wellbeing in alternative education. In F. McCallum & D. Price (eds), *Nurturing wellbeing development in education: From little things big things grow*. London: Routledge, pp. 72–87.

Blenkiron, P. (2013) *Cognitive behavioural therapy*. Available from www.rcpsych.ac.uk/mental-healthinformation/therapies/cognitivebehaviouraltherapy.aspx, accessed 23 January 2014.

Bosworth, K., Espelage, D., DuBay, T., Daytner, G. & Karageorge, K. (2000) Preliminary evaluation of a multimedia violence prevention program for adolescents. *American Journal of Health Behavior*, 24(4), pp. 268–280.

Commonwealth of Australia (2008) *KidsMatter*. Available from www.kidsmatter.edu.au, accessed 23 January 2014.

Cross, D., Epstein, M., Hearn, L., Slee, P., Shaw, T. & Monks, H. (2011) National safe schools framework: Policy and practice to reduce bullying in Australian schools. *International Journal of Behavioral Development*, 35(5), pp. 398–404.

Emler, N. (1984) Differential involvement in delinquency: Toward an interpretation in terms of reputation management. In B.A. Maher & W.B. Maher (eds), *Progress in experimental personality research, vol. 13*. New York, NY: Academic Press, pp. 173–237.

Farrington, D.P. & Ttofi, M.M. (2009) Reducing school bullying: Evidence-based implications for policy. *Crime and Justice*, 38(1), pp. 281–345.

Faubert, B. (2012) *A literature review of school practices to overcome school failure (OECD education working papers, No. 68)*. Paris: OECD.

Green, D.M. (2015) An investigation of persistent bullying at school: Multiple perspectives of a complex social phenomenon. Doctoral dissertation, University of South Australia.

Hobbs, L.J. & Yan, Z. (2008) Cracking the walnut: Using a computer game to impact cognition, emotion, and behavior of highly aggressive fifth grade students. *Computers in Human Behavior*, 24(2), pp. 421–438.

Horner, R.H., Todd, A.W., Lewis-Palmer, T., Irvin, L.K., Sugai, G. & Boland, J.B. (2004) The school-wide evaluation tool (SET) a research instrument for assessing school-wide positive behavior support. *Journal of Positive Behavior Interventions*, 6(1), pp. 3–12.

Hymel, S., Rocke-Henderson, N. & Bonanno, R.A. (2005) Moral disengagement: A framework for understanding bullying among adolescents. *Journal of Social Sciences*, 8(1), pp. 1–11.

Jimerson, S.R., Swearer, S.M. & Espelage, D.L. (2010) International scholarship advances science and practice addressing bullying in schools. In S.R. Jimerson, S.M. Swearer & D.L. Espelage (eds), *Handbook of bullying in schools: An international perspective*. New York, NY: Routledge, pp. 1–16.

Johnson, B. & Sullivan, A. (2014) Against the tide: Enacting respectful student behaviour polices in 'get tough' time. Paper presented at the *Annual Meeting of the American Educational Research Association*, Philadelphia, PA, April 3–7.

Kowalski, R.M., Giumetti, G.W., Schroeder, A.N. & Lattanner, M.R. (2014) Bullying in the digital age: A critical review and meta-analysis of cyberbullying research among youth. *Psychological Bulletin*, 140(4). Available from http://dx.doi.org/10.1037/a0035618, accessed 23 January 2014.

Kumpulainen, K., Räsänen, E. & Henttonen, I. (1999) Children involved in bullying: Psychological disturbance and the persistence of the involvement. *Child Abuse & Neglect*, 23(12), pp. 1253–1262.

Menesini, E., Sanchez, V., Fonzi, A., Ortega, R., Costabile, A. & LoFeudo, G. (2003) Moral emotions and bullying: A cross-national comparison of differences between bullies, victims and outsiders. *Aggressive Behavior*, 29(6), pp. 515–530.

Merton, R.K. (1948) The self-fulfilling prophecy. *The Antioch Review*, 8(2), pp. 193–210.

North, R.J. & Swann, W.B. (2009) Self-verification 360°: Illuminating the light and dark sides. *Self and Identity*, 8(2–3), pp. 131–146.

Orpinas, P. & Horne, A.M. (2006) *Bullying prevention: Creating a positive school climate and developing social competence.* Washington, DC: American Psychological Association.

Pepler, D.J., Jiang, D., Craig, W.M. & Connolly, J. (2008) Developmental trajectories of bullying and associated factors. *Child Development*, 79(2), pp. 325–338.

Price, D. (2016) Wellbeing in disability education. In F. McCallum & D. Price (eds), *Nurturing wellbeing development in education: From little things big things grow.* London: Routledge, pp. 40–71.

Price, D. & McCallum, F. (2016) Leading and empowering lifelong wellbeing: Well educators, well learners, well communities. In F. McCallum & D. Price (eds), *Nurturing wellbeing development in education: From little things big things grow.* London: Routledge, pp. 133–145.

Price, D., Green, D.M., Spears, B., Scrimgeour, M., Barnes, A., Geer, R. & Johnson, B. (2014) A qualitative exploration of cyber-bystanders and moral engagement. *Australian Journal of Guidance and Counselling*, 24(1), pp. 1–17.

Rigby, K. (2002) *A meta-evaluation of methods and approaches to reducing bullying in pre-schools and early primary school in Australia.* Commonwealth Attorney-General's Department, Canberra, ACT.

Rigby, K. (2010) *Bullying interventions in schools: Six basic approaches.* Camberwell, VIC: ACER Press.

Rigby, K. (2011) What can schools do about cases of bullying? *Pastoral Care in Education*, 29(4), pp. 273–285.

Riordan, G. (2006) Reducing student 'suspension rates' and engaging students in learning: Principal and teacher approaches that work. *Improving Schools*, 9(3), pp. 239–250.

Salmivalli, C., Kaukiainen, A. & Voeten, M. (2005) Anti-bullying intervention: Implementation and outcome. *British Journal of Educational Psychology*, 75(3), pp. 465–487.

Shaughnessy, J. (2012) The challenge for English schools in responding to current debates on behaviour and violence. *Pastoral Care in Education*, 30(2), pp. 87–97.

Slee, P.T., Lawson, M.J., Russell, A., Askell-Williams, H., Dix, K.L., Owens, L.D., Skrzypiec, G. & Spears, B. (2009) *KidsMatter primary evaluation final report.* Melbourne, VIC: Beyond Blue.

Smith, P.K. & Shu, S. (2000) What good schools can do about bullying: Findings from a survey in English schools after a decade of research and action. *Childhood*, 7(2), pp. 193–212.

Spears, B. & Kofoed, J. (2013) Transgressing research binaries. In P. Smith & G. Steffgen (eds), *Cyberbullying through the new media: Findings from an international network.* New York, NY: Psychology Press, 201–221.

Taddeo, C.M., Spears, B., Ey, L.-A., Green, D.M., Price, D.A., Carslake, T. & Cox, G.E. (2015) *A report on the evaluation of the Safe Schools Hub.* Adelaide, SA: University of South Australia.

Ttofi, M.M. & Farrington, D.P. (2011) Effectiveness of school-based programs to reduce bullying: A systematic and meta-analytic review. *Journal of Experimental Criminology*, 7(1), pp. 27–56.

INDEX

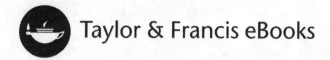